# Real Food
# SLOW COOKER
## SUPPERS

# Real Food
# SLOW COOKER
# SUPPERS

### EASY, FAMILY-FRIENDLY RECIPES FROM SCRATCH

## Samantha Skaggs
founder of the blog FiveHeartHome.com

PAGE STREET
PUBLISHING CO.

PAGE STREET
PUBLISHING CO.

First published in 2016 by

Page Street Publishing Co.

27 Congress Street, Suite 103

Salem, MA 01970

www.pagestreetpublishing.com

Distributed by Macmillan, sales in Canada by The Canadian Manda Group.

19  18   17  16    1  2  3  4  5

ISBN-13: 9781624142659

ISBN-10: 1624142656

Library of Congress Control Number: 2016935689

Cover and book design by Page Street Publishing Co.

Photography by Samantha Skaggs

Printed and bound in China

Page Street is proud to be a member of 1% for the Planet. Members donate 1 percent of their sales to one or more of the over 1,500 environmental and sustainability charities across the globe who participate in this program.

## TO JASON, GRANT, REID AND ANNIE-

I love you all so much, and I'm thankful for you every day.
Y'all are my world.

# Contents

# SOUP'S ON! - 79

# STEWS, CHILIS AND CHOWDERS - 111

# SANDWICHES, TACOS AND WRAPS - 137

# HOLIDAY HELPERS - 171

# HOMEMADE SEASONINGS AND STOCKS - 192

# INTRODUCTION

Several years back—as a sleep-deprived, stay-at-home mama of three kiddos under the age of five—I had this crazy idea to start a food blog. I loved cooking, I loved photography, I loved writing and I was yearning for a creative outlet to prove to myself that my tired, fuzzy, baby-saturated brain could still function well enough to form a coherent written sentence. But what to call this new venture? Well, it hit me while folding socks in the laundry room one day, inspired by the mountain of dirty clothes created by five beloved family members.

From the beginning, I had no interest in *Five Heart Home* representing anything that I wasn't. As much as I enjoyed creating and cooking for my family, I was a busy mom with needy young children, and I didn't have a lot of time to spend in the kitchen. On the other hand, I was intent on feeding my kids wholesome, homemade food made from real ingredients. So that's exactly how my blog started, and that's how it remains today—quick and easy, family-friendly, real-food recipes.

With babies, toddlers and now older kids, the slow cooker has always been a central figure in my life when it comes to consistently getting dinner on the table. I appreciate that I can choose a recipe that fits my schedule—whether that means prepping a meal the night before, first thing in the morning or midway through the day—so that there's not much left to do come dinnertime. However, I've always felt a little frustrated that so many slow cooker recipes are rife with processed ingredients, from condensed soups to dried seasoning packets.

And so, when I found myself presented with the amazing opportunity to create an entire cookbook of from-scratch slow cooker recipes using real, unprocessed ingredients, I jumped at the chance. It's exactly the kind of cookbook that I myself have always wanted to cook from, with a wide variety of straightforward, creative, flavorful recipes . . . that don't all end up tasting like the same thing, as slow cooker recipes often do.

Working on *Real Food Slow Cooker Suppers* has been a true labor of love, and my greatest wish is that it is deemed helpful by all of you who use it. I hope that these recipes make your taste buds happy and your life easier. I hope that this cookbook empowers you and your family to eat healthier, inspires you to try new things and brings your loved ones 'round the dinner table together.

So dive in and meet me by the slow cooker! And any time you're on the hunt for even more easy, yummy, real-food recipes, I'd be thrilled to have you stop by and say hi over at FiveHeartHome.com.

*Samantha Skaggs*

# SLOW COOKER BASICS

## MODERN-DAY SLOW COOKERS, REAL-FOOD INGREDIENTS AND GETTING TO KNOW YOUR SLOW COOKER

The slow cooker is a magical kitchen appliance. It allows you to prepare a meal ahead of time, when you actually *have* time, and then conveniently walk away until dinnertime. It provides a low, slow cooking environment that's perfect for turning out tender ingredients that are infused with flavor. And with the right recipes, it's possible to get fabulous flavor out of a slow cooker—which is where this cookbook comes in (hint, hint)!

It's important to note that slow cooker use has evolved over the years, however. Slow cooker suppers of the past meant tossing some things into the slow cooker in the morning—usually, processed ingredients like canned condensed soups and seasoning packets—and then letting 'em cook all day long.

But two things have changed. For food safety reasons, newer model slow cookers are designed to cook hotter than they used to. This means that if you follow an old slow cooker recipe using a new slow cooker, your food is likely going to overcook. It also means that the era of cooking just about any type of slow cooker recipe for eight to ten hours is over (or at least it's dwindling, as older model slow cookers gradually go kaput).

The other factor that has changed is the modern-day cook. As people become more in tune with the foods they're eating and what they're feeding their families, the stereotypically processed slow cooker ingredients of the past are making way for fresh, real-food ingredients. And while that is terrific news on the health front, it also means a small loss as far as convenience. After all, plopping a can of condensed soup into the slow cooker was as simple as opening up a can. Making your own sauce to replace that soup takes several ingredients and at least a few minutes. But lucky for us, the trade-off is well worth a healthier, fresher, better tasting meal, and real-food slow cooker suppers can still be relatively quick and easy to make.

All of the recipes in this cookbook were tested in and created for a modern (i.e., hotter running), large, oval, 6- to 7-quart (5- to 6-L) slow cooker. While there is a bit of wiggle room as far as size for many of the recipes, certain recipes must be made in a large, oval slow cooker or they literally won't work (primarily because the ingredients won't fit). Those recipes, such as Cheesy Spinach Lasagna (page 64) or Honey-Garlic Baby Back Ribs (page 63), will indicate in the directions that the slow cooker should be large and oval-shaped.

Given the wide range of slow cookers in use these days—from older models to newer ones—I could pretty much tell y'all to cook a given recipe anywhere from two to eight hours, and for people using different slow cookers, the extremes of that time range would be accurate! But since that's too broad of a cooking time span for a given recipe, know this: the recipes in this cookbook give an average cooking time range for a modern-day slow cooker. If you have an older, cooler running slow cooker, it's very likely that you will have to cook almost all of the recipes in this cookbook for longer than the suggested time in order to achieve tender, cooked-through ingredients. And as long as you're aware of that and prepared for the extra cooking time, that's okay!

If you have a newer slow cooker that cooks more quickly, you should know that the entire time range suggested in a recipe still may not apply to you. In other words, if a recipe says to cook chicken for four to six hours, that doesn't mean that *your* chicken in *your* slow cooker will necessarily turn out perfect at four hours *as well as* five hours *and* six hours. At four hours, your chicken might be underdone and at six hours it might be dried out, so five hours would be your optimal cooking time in *your* slow cooker for that type of recipe. But your mom might make the same recipe and find that her chicken is perfectly done at four hours and starts to dry out immediately after that. And your neighbor across the street might cook the recipe to find that her chicken wasn't tender or cooked through until a full six hours had passed.

All of this slow cooker rambling is not meant to intimidate or discourage you. It simply boils down to the most important message in this cookbook: *get to know your slow cooker.* Once you do, you'll know what to expect from recipes, whether that means you should check for doneness a bit early or plan on cooking things longer than called for. So on your first go with a particular recipe or type of recipe, make a note of the exact optimal cooking time for future reference. And if your dish cooks a little quicker than expected, relax! The warm setting is your friend.

## MY FAVORITE KITCHEN TOOLS TO ENHANCE YOUR SLOW COOKER'S PERFORMANCE

Making smooth, creamy soups in the slow cooker is a hundred times easier using an **immersion blender**. While it's possible to transfer soup to a blender or food processor, purée it and then transfer it back to the slow cooker, this process can be very tedious, not to mention messy and potentially dangerous when a blender full of hot tomato soup explodes all over the kitchen (not that I have firsthand experience with this or anything). I'm telling you, a trusty immersion blender is worth its weight in gold!

This cookbook will teach you how to cook things like salmon and turkey breast and Cornish hens and pork loin in the slow cooker. How fun! *However.* All of those foods can be tricky to cook to an ideal temperature whereby the food is safe to eat but not overcooked and dried out. Therefore, I would consider a **digital meat thermometer with an oven-safe probe** that can stay in the meat the entire time it's in the slow cooker to be a must-have if you plan on making recipes other than stew, chili or pot roast in your slow cooker.

A recipe for pulled chicken sandwiches is not going to turn out as expected if it calls for 2 pounds (907 g) of chicken breasts but 3 pounds (1360 g) are accidentally used instead. The excess chicken will absorb too much sauce and the recipe will turn out dry. Therefore, I highly recommend investing in a small, inexpensive **digital food scale**. There's no need to go crazy and measure everything, but if you're not sure how many randomly sized potatoes make a pound (450 g), it's better to pull out the food scale than end up using way too many.

Slow cooker recipes often take advantage of more marbled cuts of meat because these cuts turn melt-in-your-mouth tender with long, slow cooking. This means that the resulting gravies and sauces are often topped with a layer of melted fat that needs to be removed. While the recipes in this cookbook recommend using a spoon to skim the fat from the surface of the cooking liquids, that task is actually much easier if you have a handy **fat separator**.

And finally, I love a **sharp pair of kitchen shears** when preparing meats for the slow cooker. Kitchen shears are ideal for trimming the fat off of chicken thighs, cutting chicken breasts into cubes, snipping raw bacon into small pieces and so much more.

## GENERAL SLOW COOKER (AND COOKING) TIPS

If you're not certain whether a cut of meat is fully cooked after cooking in the slow cooker, measuring the internal temperature with a food thermometer is the only way to know for sure. You cannot always judge the doneness of certain slow cooker recipes by the interior color of the meat. Because of chemical changes in the meat that occur during slow cooking, sometimes certain types of meat such as turkey breast or ground beef can retain a pinkish hue even after they have been fully cooked to a safe temperature. So if your meatballs still look pink inside even after you've cooked the heck out of them, stick an instant-read thermometer into the center of one (just do so quickly before its temperature starts to drop). As long as the temperature has reached the recommendation listed in the recipe, the meat is fully cooked and safe to eat, despite its color.

Weight is your best basis for measurement when it comes to determining how much of an ingredient is needed for a recipe (like chicken breasts, potatoes and so on), since their sizes can vary so widely, as can different people's perceptions of those sizes. If you don't have a scale, at least use the net weight of the package or bag of produce that you purchase to approximately guesstimate the correct amount to use.

Dry ingredients should always be measured by *weight*, not volume. In other words, 8 ounces = 1 cup *only when measuring liquids*.

For example, cheese is a dry ingredient. When you shred cheese and measure out 1 cup (121 g), that does not equal 8 ounces (227 g) of cheese, since cheese is measured by weight, not liquid volume. If you weigh that cup of cheese, it actually measures 4 ounces (121 g). So a recipe in this cookbook will give the correct equivalents, such as "1 cup (4 oz [121 g]) shredded cheese," even though at first glance, those equivalents may seem off.

When an ingredient is listed in a recipe, the order in which it's written from left to right is important, and pay particular attention to commas. "½ cup (70 g) olives, chopped" means that you'll need to measure ½ cup (70 g) olives and then chop them. "½ cup (90 g) chopped olives" means that you'll need to chop the olives first and then measure out ½ cup (90 g).

I tend to avoid browning or searing meat before adding it to the slow cooker unless I feel that the result is worth the extra time and the extra pot to wash. If it really makes a difference to the final flavor of the dish, I'll include searing in the directions (as with Chicken and Dumplings [page 116] and Beef Bourguignon [page 124]). However, if I leave out the step of pre-browning but you prefer to sear anyway, feel free to do so!

Many slow cooker recipes can be prepped the night before. You can trim and cube meat, chop veggies, measure out spices and dry ingredients, whip up sauces and more. After prepping any ingredients, simply put them in containers and refrigerate them overnight (or store them on the counter, if appropriate). The next morning, transfer the ingredients to the slow cooker, turn it on and you're done!

Never refrigerate a slow cooker insert full of prepped ingredients, however. Sudden temperature changes can cause the ceramic insert to crack, which could occur if you ever put a chilled insert into the slow cooker base and turn on the heat. For the same reason, if you need to add hot liquids such as a sauce made on the stove to the slow cooker, allow those liquids to cool a bit before pouring them in.

Speaking of food temperature, it's also important to cook only fully thawed foods in the slow cooker. Cooking ingredients from their frozen state can prevent them from reaching a safe, bacteria-killing temperature quickly enough in the slow cooker.

If a slow cooker recipe only gives directions for cooking on low heat, that's because that temperature yields optimal results for that particular combination of ingredients. If you choose to cook the recipe for less time on high heat, the final dish may not turn out as moist or tender, given your particular slow cooker.

If you prefer a thinner consistency, soups and stews can always be thinned out with additional liquid like broth or dairy products at the end of the cooking time. Along the same lines, the consistency of leftovers will often thicken up once refrigerated, so a splash of liquid may need to be added for reheating.

Flavors within a recipe can mellow and change as a slow cooker does its job, so it's always important to check and adjust seasonings at the end of a recipe's cooking time. Almost always, you will need to add additional salt and pepper to really make the flavors pop. If a recipe needs more salt at the end, I stir it in ¼ teaspoon at a time, tasting at each interval, until the flavor is just right.

## HOW SPECIFIC INGREDIENTS PERFORM IN A SLOW COOKER AND MY RECOMMENDATIONS FOR WHAT WORKS BEST

**Chicken** can cook beautifully in a slow cooker, but certain cuts do dry out more easily than others. Boneless, skinless chicken breasts are most prone to drying out and therefore require the shortest cooking time of any kind of chicken. Boneless, skinless chicken thighs may take a bit longer to cook than breasts, but they typically stay moister. Bone-in chicken pieces are the best at retaining moisture and therefore can withstand longer cooking times, which is why these are used in soups that include other longer-cooking ingredients like beans or potatoes.

In certain recipes, I like to leave the skin on the chicken. It can add flavor to soups (being discarded before serving), or it can be broiled until crispy at the end of certain recipes (such as Barbecue-Sauce Chicken Thighs [page 38] or Garlic "Roasted" Whole Chicken [page 184]). Even in such recipes, you can always remove the skin before cooking if that's your preference.

If a recipe specifies a certain cut of chicken (such as chicken thighs in the Chicken Caesar Sandwiches [page 166]), it's because that's what I found to yield optimal results in that particular recipe. If a recipe gives options for chicken cuts, any of those will work well—just mind the cooking time depending on which cut you use. I actually enjoy using both chicken breasts and thighs together in some recipes, such as soups or pulled chicken sandwiches, as the combination adds moisture and flavor. However, I always prefer slow cooking chicken on low heat, which is why high heat is not typically given as an option in chicken recipes. It can be done, of course, but it is much more likely to result in stringy, dry, overcooked chicken.

When cooking a larger piece of poultry—such as a turkey breast, whole chicken or Cornish hens—it is highly advisable to use a meat thermometer to test the doneness of the bird in both the breast and the thighs. Even if the breast tests done, the thighs may not be fully cooked at the same time. Keep in mind that color does not always indicate doneness of meat cooked in a slow cooker; for example, your turkey breast may have a tinge of pink even after a safe temperature has been reached. Using a thermometer is the only way to ensure that certain poultry has been properly cooked. Also, the juices should run clear, not pink, where the bird's leg pulls away from the body.

**Beef** is one of my favorite things to cook in the slow cooker. Since beef often means larger, more marbled pieces of meat, it's usually less persnickety in the slow cooker than chicken and can withstand longer cooking times and higher temperatures.

My preferred cut of beef for the slow cooker is boneless chuck roast. It has a good amount of marbling running through it, which makes it moist and tender after a long stint in the slow cooker. I typically trim it before cooking and then skim the gravy or slow cooker liquids to remove the fat that has melted while the roast cooked.

I like to use chuck roast for pot roast recipes, shredded beef sandwiches and cut into cubes for stews and chilis. Cubing a roast, however, can take some time, as trimming and cutting the beef into chunks can be rather labor-intensive. I prefer cubing my own chuck roast in order to control the quality of meat in my stew or chili, and I will oftentimes trim and cube my beef the night before making a recipe so that in the morning all I have to do is toss it into the slow cooker. However, when I'm short on time, I sometimes substitute precut beef stew meat as a shortcut ingredient in recipes calling for cubed beef chuck roast. When doing so, I always consider that some packaged beef stew meat hasn't been trimmed very carefully, making for a less enjoyable dining experience later. So I typically only buy beef stew meat when it looks well-trimmed.

I keep in mind that when a recipe calls for 2 ½ pounds (1134 g) of chuck roast cut into cubes, the recipe is taking into account the fact that a percentage of that weight is the marbling that will be discarded before the beef is added to the slow cooker. So if I'm going to buy beef stew meat instead, I buy slightly less (closer to 2 pounds [907 g]) to account for the fact that there won't be as much meat to discard.

**Brisket** is another cut of meat that does well in the slow cooker. And for lean beef cutlets, I prefer a **boneless beef top round roast** cut into slices.

**Pork** can be very versatile in the slow cooker. You can either cook a large, well-marbled cut such as pork butt roast for a long period of time until it's fall-apart tender, or you can cook a lean cut of pork such as pork loin or pork chops for a shorter period of time, while carefully monitoring the temperature so as not to overcook.

A **pork butt roast** is my favorite cut of pork to use for slow cooker stews, chilis and pulled pork. The name of the cut can be confusing, however, because it actually comes from the shoulder of the pig. It is sometimes called a Boston butt roast or a shoulder roast. Much like a beef chuck roast, I always try to remove large sections of marbling from a pork butt roast before adding it to the slow cooker, and I skim melted fat from the liquids in the slow cooker at the end of the cooking time. Other marbled pork roasts may be substituted in recipes calling for pork butt roast. Just don't use something like a pork loin roast in that type of recipe, which is much leaner and will turn out too dry.

Sometimes I will use **boneless country-style pork ribs** for a pulled pork–type recipe instead of a pork butt roast, particularly if I need a smaller quantity of pork. Boneless country-style pork ribs are not actually ribs—they're more like boneless pork chops—and if they're not already in the meat case, you may have to ask the butcher for them.

When it comes to preparing **pork loin** in the slow cooker, a short, thick pork loin works better than a long, skinny pork loin since the former cooks slower and longer. If your pork loin is on the skinnier side or your slow cooker runs hot, your pork loin may reach 145°F (63°C) on the shorter end of the cooking time. That's okay—just keep an eye on a pork loin recipe the first time you make it. Because pork loin is so lean (like chicken breast), it's really easy to overcook it, which causes it to become dry. I highly recommend keeping an oven-safe digital thermometer inserted in the meat the entire time it cooks.

**Shrimp** is a delicious addition to a variety of slow cooker recipes. However, since attaining a pleasing texture for shrimp requires precise cooking times (and slow cookers aren't exactly precise because of variations in temperature), I've learned that boiling fresh shrimp separately on the stove and then adding it to the already-cooked recipe in the slow cooker at the last minute yields the best texture and the most consistent results.

Cooking **dried beans** in the slow cooker is pretty much effortless. Because of long cooking times, soaking the beans ahead of time is typically not necessary. However, any time you make a slow cooker dried bean–based recipe for the first time, it's a good idea to keep an eye on the liquid level as the recipe cooks and stir in a bit more broth if the beans end up absorbing too much.

Also, it's very important to note that old beans may never end up softening, no matter how long you cook them! Always buy fresh dried beans for best results and if they still take an abnormally long time to soften, it's possible that they were stored in the warehouse for a long time before they ever made it to the store. Also, adding salt to beans at the beginning of the cooking time can inhibit the beans from adequately softening, so it's always best to salt toward the end of the cooking process.

Different types of **potatoes** can be used fairly interchangeably in the slow cooker, although the variety that yields the best results in individual recipes is always listed. I recommend peeling russet potatoes before adding them to the slow cooker. Yellow and red potatoes have a thinner skin, so sometimes I peel them (as in a soup) and sometimes I leave the skin on (to accompany a pot roast). The "to peel or not to peel" recommendation is always given in a recipe, but it's also a matter of personal preference.

As far as potato size, it can be quite variable, which is why I recommend weighing potatoes with a scale to determine how many you need to use.

**Onions** can add great flavor to slow cooker recipes, but they can also be pungent if too many are used or they're not cooked long enough. That's why the recipes in this cookbook sometimes only require half an onion, and they only call for onions when the cooking time is long enough. Yellow onions are my preference, as they become the mellowest in the slow cooker. If you wish, you can always sauté onions for a few minutes before adding them to the slow cooker to bring out their sweetness.

**Jalapeños** can be used to impart heat and flavor to a variety of recipes. If your family's tastes run mild, simply use a spoon to scrape out and discard the seeds and membranes before dicing the jalapeño. Or you may retain the jalapeño seeds in a recipe for extra heat. Also keep in mind that jalapeños and other spicy ingredients will become milder over long cooking times.

When a recipe in this cookbook calls for cloves of **garlic**, it is referring to *large* cloves, but not those abnormally giant ones known as elephant garlic.

Cooking with **wine** and **beer** adds depth of flavor to slow cooker recipes. You are always free to substitute chicken broth or beef broth (depending on which one better fits the recipe) for wine or beer, but keep in mind that the final flavors of the recipe will not be as complex. Most of the time, the actual flavor of the wine and beer cannot be detected in the final recipe. However, in a couple of recipes, such as Chicken Cordon Bleu Soup (page 87) and Beef Bourguignon (page 124), a greater amount of wine is used because its flavor is a signature component of the dish.

Since I cook with wine a lot but don't necessarily want to open a new bottle every time, I keep a four-pack of decent but not expensive mini wine bottles from the grocery store on hand. That way, when I only need a small amount of wine for a recipe, I can open one mini bottle, pour out what I need, screw the lid back on and place the bottle in the refrigerator without taking up too much room until I make another recipe calling for that wine. I usually keep mini bottles of Chardonnay or Pinot Grigio on hand for when I need white wine in a recipe and Merlot or Pinot Noir for when I need red wine.

Cooking with beer can add amazing depth of flavor to chili, stew and taco meat, but you do need to use the right kind of beer. I prefer amber or dark lager in most recipes (unless another kind is specified), which for me almost always means Negra Modelo for Tex-Mex and Mexican recipes or Shiner Bock for general cooking.

Medium-dry or dry sherry is another secret flavor booster that can be added in small quantities at the end of certain recipes, usually soups. Dry sherry is *not* the same as cooking sherry, which is often loaded with extra sodium and fillers. A bottle of dry sherry will keep indefinitely in your pantry and while adding it to recipes is optional, it really does something nice for the flavor. Just be aware that you don't need much—a tiny bit goes a long way, so add it slowly if you're not sure how you'll like it.

**Canned tomatoes** are a common ingredient in slow cooker recipes. Some brands of canned tomatoes are more acidic than others, so it's always possible that you may have to add a tiny bit of sugar to counter any acidity still present at the end of the recipe. The recipes in this cookbook call for fire-roasted diced or crushed tomatoes, because they contribute more flavor to dishes that have long cooking times. However, if you can only find regular diced tomatoes, those will work just fine. In Italian-inspired recipes, I prefer using San Marzano canned tomatoes if available. And finally, I always try to buy canned tomatoes in cans with BPA-free lining when I can find them, which, happily, is becoming more and more common.

**Chipotle peppers in adobo sauce** are a fabulous ingredient for adding smoky heat to chili and a variety of Mexican-influenced recipes. Chipotles in adobo can be found in the Mexican foods section of most grocery stores. If you're looking for flavor as opposed to heat, be sure to scrape and remove the seeds from the center of the chipotles (where most of the heat is found) before mincing them. Since chipotles are spicy, you can always start out using just half of a scraped pepper or maybe a tiny bit of adobo sauce until you gauge your comfort level with the heat. Since you will probably never use a whole can of chipotles in a given recipe, you can store the leftovers in a glass container in the refrigerator to be used in another upcoming recipe. Or you can freeze individual peppers plus a dollop of adobo sauce in an ice cube tray and then pop out the cubes and store them in a freezer bag until needed.

For a comparable flavor and heat level to chipotles in adobo, **chipotle chile powder** (sometimes labled as chipotle chile pepper powder) is sometimes used in chili and Tex-Mex recipes instead. This spice is basically just ground-up, smoke-dried jalapeño peppers, not quite as hot as cayenne pepper but definitely spicy. It is not to be confused with **chili powder**, which is a common spice blend that is much milder.

I used **fine sea salt** (I prefer Redmond Real Salt brand) when creating recipes for this cookbook, but regular table salt will work just fine in equivalent amounts.

Different types of **cooking oils** are often recommended for different purposes. I prefer using extra-virgin olive oil in marinades and dressings. Searing requires an oil with a higher smoke point, which can mean a very good quality olive oil, but more typically, a neutral vegetable oil like canola.

Since any **butter** in this cookbook is typically not used for baking, and it's not usually used in great amounts, you can use salted or unsalted butter—whatever you keep on hand—unless a recipe specifies otherwise.

To use **Greek yogurt** in a cold sauce such as tzatziki, you may choose between full-fat, low-fat or fat-free yogurt, depending on your preference. When stirring Greek yogurt into a slow cooker soup or cooked sauce, I recommend using full-fat Greek yogurt. Greek yogurt as well as **sour cream** will need to be tempered before adding it to the hot slow cooker so as to prevent curdling (specific directions are included in each recipe).

Most of the time, if I want to finish off a recipe with liquid dairy to add creaminess and a touch of decadence, I use **half-and-half**, which is a nice middle ground. However, you may always substitute heavy cream for a richer outcome or whole milk to make things lighter. I don't recommend low-fat or fat-free milk since they won't really lend any creaminess. If you don't have half-and-half, you may substitute a mixture of half heavy cream and half whole milk in its place, which is where it gets the name half-and-half in the first place.

Sometimes the type of **mustard** used in a recipe can be confusing. "Prepared yellow mustard" refers to a bottle of the liquid stuff, while "mustard powder" refers to the dried spice. If a recipe calls for Dijon or stone-ground mustard, those are the prepared varieties.

Most of the time I use dried **herbs** in slow cooker recipes. However, for certain dishes, I use minced fresh herbs, particularly when stirring them in toward the end of a recipe for a pop of freshness and flavor. If I recommend fresh herbs in a recipe, it's because I think they make a difference. Standard herb conversions are:

3 parts fresh = 1 part dried

So 3 teaspoons (3 g) minced fresh thyme leaves is equivalent to 1 teaspoon (1 g) dried thyme leaves.

## SPECIAL TIPS AND TRICKS IN THIS COOKBOOK

To make my own **breadcrumbs**, I usually save the undesirable (or so say my kids) end pieces from loaves of bread in a plastic bag in the refrigerator. Then when I have enough, I grind them up in the food processor or blender. If there are leftover breadcrumbs after I make a recipe, I store them in the freezer to use for future recipes. But you can definitely use a tub of dried breadcrumbs from the store instead of making your own—just try to find an all-natural brand that doesn't include processed ingredients like hydrogenated oils or high-fructose corn syrup.

To save leftover **tomato paste** from a half-used can, measure the tomato paste onto a wax paper–lined baking sheet in tablespoon-sized dollops and freeze until they are solid. Peel the tomato paste blobs from the wax paper, pop them in a freezer bag, and store them in the freezer until needed for future recipes.

Instead of chopping fresh basil, you can turn it into ribbons of **chiffonade**. Simply stack washed and dried basil leaves on top of one another, tightly roll them lengthwise like a cigar, and use a sharp knife to slice them crosswise into thin ribbons.

Using a fat separator or skimming the settled cooking liquids with a large spoon are the recommended and preferred methods for removing fat from the surface of broths, sauces and gravies. However, if a thick layer of melted fat is visibly sitting on top of the cooking liquids, I use an easy paper towel trick to remove at least some of it. I lay a paper towel directly on the surface of the cooking liquid and then immediately lift it back up so that only the fat has time to soak in, quickly disposing of it in a very nearby waiting receptacle. I then repeat as necessary until most of the fat has been removed. Or, if I see small pockets of melted fat, I very quickly dab the edge of a paper towel directly on top of them. This trick doesn't work with all recipes, as sometimes the paper towel lifts up too much sauce in addition to the fat, and sometimes there's just too much fat to begin with. But if the paper towel gets soaked with clear fat and little to no sauce, that's when I like to use this trick.

# DINNERTIME CLASSICS

## Fourteen Classic Recipes Made Over for the Better

When the concept for this cookbook was conceived, I thought it would be fun to take a variety of classic main dish recipes and see if I could convert them to the slow cooker. In some cases, these recipes already existed in slow cooker land, but they were rife with canned condensed soups and store-bought seasoning packets, and I was determined to convert them to dishes that relied on real-food ingredients instead.

So in this chapter, you get the classics. If beef is your thing, there's fall-apart Comforting Pot Roast (page 22) in a flavorful gravy with root veggies. I'm pretty sure my kids could happily eat Cheeseburger Macaroni (page 41) every single night. Hearty Beef Ragu (page 26) over creamy polenta is Italian comfort food at its finest. And did you know that you can even make tender, homemade Swedish Meatballs (page 29) in the slow cooker?

Chicken options are as American as Barbecue-Sauce Chicken Thighs (page 38). But this popular poultry also takes on an ethnic spin, from Asian-inspired Cashew Chicken (page 30) to Indian Butter Chicken (page 45) to Paella (page 49), which also features sausage and shrimp.

And for the pork lovers out there, there are simple, effective tips to ensure that your Marinated Pork Chops and Potatoes (page 34) turn out tender and juicy. So what are you waiting for? Break out the slow cooker and serve up a classic tonight!

# COMFORTING POT ROAST

When it comes to a stick-to-your-ribs, meat-and-potatoes kind of meal, it's hard to beat the humble pot roast. Juicy, tender beef, flavorful gravy, fall-apart veggies . . . nope, it never gets old. Some people feel obliged to sear their roast before popping it into the slow cooker, and while you can certainly do that with this recipe should you so desire, I honestly don't think it's necessary. There are plenty of herbs, spices and natural flavorings here to give your pot roast amazing flavor without the extra step, time and dirty pot of searing. As for the gravy? It's so good, I made sure there's plenty, which comes in handy for reheating any leftovers. Or drowning the potatoes on your plate. Or slurping it up with a spoon.

YIELD: 6 SERVINGS

1 ½ tbsp (18 g) House Seasoning (page 193)

2 tsp (2 g) dried parsley

½ tsp dried oregano

½ tsp dried thyme

¼ tsp dried basil

¼ tsp dried rosemary

¼ tsp dried sage

3 ½ to 4 lb (1.6 to 1.8 kg) boneless beef chuck roast, trimmed

4 cloves garlic, minced

2 lb (910 kg) small red potatoes, unpeeled and left whole (or cut into chunks if using larger potatoes)

1 lb (455 g) baby carrots

2 cups (480 ml) low-sodium beef broth

2 tbsp (30 ml) balsamic vinegar

2 tbsp (30 ml) Worcestershire sauce

1 tbsp (17 g) tomato paste

2 tbsp (16 g) cornstarch plus 2 tbsp (30 ml) water

Salt and freshly ground black pepper, to taste

In a small bowl, combine the House Seasoning, parsley, oregano, thyme, basil, rosemary and sage. Season the roast by evenly sprinkling both sides with the herb mixture and rubbing it into the meat. Place the seasoned roast in a large slow cooker and arrange the garlic, potatoes and carrots around it and on top.

In a medium bowl, whisk together the beef broth, balsamic vinegar, Worcestershire sauce and tomato paste and pour over the contents of the slow cooker. Cover the slow cooker and cook on low for 8 to 10 hours, or on high for 5 to 6 hours, until the roast and vegetables are tender.

Transfer the roast and the vegetables to a serving platter; cover them with foil to keep them warm. Use a large spoon to skim excess fat from the surface of the pan juices in the slow cooker, then strain the pan juices through a fine-mesh sieve into a medium saucepan over medium-high heat. Bring the pan juices to a boil, then reduce to a simmer.

In a small bowl, mix the cornstarch and the water until smooth. Continuously whisk the pan juices in the saucepan while slowly pouring in the cornstarch slurry. Allow the mixture to simmer, stirring occasionally, and cook for 1 to 2 minutes, until the gravy is thickened. Season the gravy with salt and pepper to taste, and serve it over the roast and vegetables.

# TERIYAKI CHICKEN BREASTS

This Asian-inspired chicken dish gets loads of flavor from a glossy homemade teriyaki sauce. It's important to use bone-in chicken breasts in this recipe to prevent the delicate white meat from drying out. That being said, if you must use boneless, skinless chicken breasts, be sure to check them early as they will cook through more quickly, taking anywhere from two to four hours. You may also substitute bone-in chicken thighs for the breasts, keeping in mind that they may take slightly longer to cook. Regardless of your choice of chicken, I recommend serving this sweet and savory meal over rice to soak up that delectable teriyaki sauce with a big green salad on the side for a complete, simple, scrumptious meal.

YIELD: 4 TO 6 SERVINGS

2 ½ to 3 lb (1.1 to 1.4 kg) bone-in chicken breasts or thighs, skin removed and trimmed

4 cloves garlic, minced

2 tbsp (19 g) minced fresh ginger

½ cup (120 ml) low-sodium soy sauce

½ cup (120 ml) honey

3 tbsp (45 ml) rice vinegar

2 tbsp (30 ml) water

¼ to ½ tsp crushed red pepper flakes

3 tbsp (24 g) cornstarch plus 3 tbsp (45 ml) water

Chopped green onions, optional, for serving

Sesame seeds, optional, for serving

Place the chicken breasts in a large slow cooker. In a medium bowl, combine the garlic, ginger, soy sauce, honey, rice vinegar, water and crushed red pepper flakes. Pour the sauce over the chicken. Cover the slow cooker and cook on low for 4 to 6 hours until the chicken is cooked through but not dry.

Carefully transfer the chicken to a plate, and tent it with foil to keep it warm. In a small bowl, mix the cornstarch and the water until smooth and set aside. Pour the liquids from the slow cooker into a medium saucepan over medium-high heat and bring to a boil. Whisk the sauce continuously while slowly pouring in the cornstarch slurry. Reduce the heat to a simmer and cook for 1 to 2 minutes, stirring constantly, until the sauce is thick and glossy. Pour the sauce over the chicken to coat it and serve leftover sauce on the side along with the green onions and sesame seeds.

# BEEF RAGU

Italian comfort food can take many forms, but rich, beefy ragu is right on up there with the best! After the roast becomes deliciously tender, it's as simple as pulling it apart and mixing it into the glorious sauce. The type of canned tomatoes you use in this recipe can affect the final outcome, so I highly recommend San Marzanos if you can find them. The grated carrot in this dish naturally counters any excessive acidity from whatever kind of tomatoes you use, but if your sauce still seems a tad too acidic by the time it's done, you can stir in a bit of sugar, ½ teaspoon at a time, until it tastes just right. Be sure to adjust the salt at the end as well to really make the flavors pop, and if you'd like a little kick, add a pinch of crushed red pepper flakes. And while a bed of pasta makes a fabulous foundation for this ragu, I think it's particularly lovely served over a bowl of creamy polenta.

YIELD: 6 TO 8 SERVINGS

½ medium yellow onion, finely chopped

6 cloves garlic, minced

2 ½ to 3 lb (1.1 to 1.4 kg) boneless beef chuck roast, trimmed

1 tbsp (12 g) House Seasoning (page 193)

Freshly ground black pepper, to taste

1 (28-oz [794-g]) can crushed tomatoes (preferably San Marzano)

1 cup (240 ml) low-sodium beef broth

3 tbsp (50 g) tomato paste

1 large carrot, peeled and grated

2 tbsp (30 ml) red wine vinegar

2 tbsp (9 g) minced fresh rosemary or 2 tsp (3 g) dried rosemary

1 ½ tsp (1 g) dried thyme

1 ½ tsp (1 g) dried oregano

½ tsp salt, plus more to taste

1 cup (160 g) uncooked polenta (Italian corn grits), prepared to a creamy consistency according to the package directions

Freshly grated or shredded Parmesan cheese, for serving

Minced fresh parsley, for serving

Scatter the onions and garlic in the bottom of a large slow cooker. Sprinkle both sides of the roast with House Seasoning and pepper and lay the roast on top of the onions and garlic.

In a medium bowl, stir together the crushed tomatoes, beef broth, tomato paste, carrot, red wine vinegar, rosemary, thyme, oregano, salt and additional pepper. Pour the tomato mixture over the top of the roast. Cover the slow cooker and cook on low for 8 to 10 hours, until the beef is very tender.

Use a large spoon to skim the fat from the surface of the sauce in the slow cooker. Use 2 forks to shred the beef directly in the slow cooker, and stir the meat into the sauce. Season to taste with additional salt and pepper, cover the slow cooker once more and cook on low for 1 hour to allow the flavors to meld.

Serve the ragu over the polenta, garnished with a generous amount of Parmesan and a sprinkle of parsley.

# SWEDISH MEATBALLS

If you've ever visited a certain large, Swedish, rat maze–like furniture store, you're probably already familiar with this next recipe. Tender and perfectly seasoned in a creamy, sour cream–kissed gravy, these meatballs are the epitome of a family-pleasing supper. Need even more reasons to make them at home? Well, not only are they easy to whip up in the slow cooker, but your dining table presumably exudes a more refined ambiance than a crowded, noisy food court. For an extra-special touch, serve your meatballs with a spoonful of lingonberry jam on the side!

YIELD: 6 TO 8 SERVINGS

### SWEDISH MEATBALLS

2 lb (910 g) lean ground beef (90 percent lean)

1 cup (120 g) unseasoned dried or fresh breadcrumbs

½ cup (120 ml) whole milk

1 tsp (6 g) salt

½ tsp onion powder

¼ tsp ground allspice

⅛ tsp ground nutmeg

Freshly ground black pepper, to taste

### GRAVY

3 cups (720 ml) low-sodium beef broth

¼ cup (30 g) all-purpose flour

2 tsp (10 ml) Worcestershire sauce

1 tsp (5 ml) apple cider vinegar

1 tbsp (12 g) House Seasoning (page 193)

⅓ cup (70 g) sour cream

Salt and freshly ground black pepper, to taste

Minced fresh parsley, for serving

Lingonberry jam, for serving

In a large bowl, thoroughly combine the ground beef, breadcrumbs, milk, salt, onion powder, allspice, nutmeg and pepper. Form the ground beef mixture into 24 equally sized meatballs. Arrange a layer of meatballs in the bottom of a large slow cooker, and add the remaining meatballs in a second layer on top.

In another large bowl, whisk together the beef broth, flour, Worcestershire sauce, apple cider vinegar and House Seasoning. Evenly pour this mixture over the meatballs in the slow cooker. Cover the slow cooker and cook on low for 8 hours, or on high for 4 hours, until the meatballs are cooked through yet still tender. Homemade meatballs cooked in the slow cooker may still look slightly pink in the center even after they are fully cooked, but they are safe to eat once they have reached an internal temperature of 160°F (74°C)—see page 14 for a more detailed explanation.

Use a slotted spoon to transfer the meatballs to a platter; cover the platter to keep the meatballs warm. Skim the fat from the surface of the gravy in the slow cooker. Measure the sour cream into a medium bowl and temper it to prevent curdling by spooning some warm gravy from the slow cooker into the sour cream and stirring well. Add more gravy to the sour cream and stir again. Repeat this process several times to gradually bring up the temperature of the sour cream. Once the sour cream is warm, pour it back into the slow cooker and stir to combine. Adjust the seasoning of the gravy with additional salt and pepper to taste.

Add the meatballs back to the slow cooker and stir to coat them with gravy. Cover the slow cooker and cook on high for 30 minutes. Sprinkle the meatballs with the parsley and serve them with the lingonberry jam.

### Samantha's Tip

To make 24 equally sized meatballs, smooth the top of the ground beef mixture in the bowl and then use a butter knife to divide it into 8 equal "slices," like a pie. Then scoop out each triangle and pinch it into 3 equal pieces. Roll the pieces into meatballs, taking care not to overwork the ground beef mixture or pack the meatballs too tightly or they won't be tender.

# CASHEW CHICKEN

Are you as obsessed with cashews as I am? If so, the next time you get a hankering for Chinese takeout, skip the fried stuff and the MSG by whipping up this effortless Cashew Chicken in the slow cooker instead. Atop a fluffy bed of rice with steamed veggies on the side, it's an easy, delicious way to enjoy Asian flavors (and lots of cashews!) at home.

YIELD: 4 TO 6 SERVINGS

2 lb (910 g) boneless, skinless chicken breasts or thighs, trimmed and cut into 1 ½-inch (4-cm) cubes

¾ cup (180 ml) low-sodium chicken broth

3 tbsp (45 ml) oyster sauce (preferably MSG-free)

3 tbsp (45 ml) low-sodium soy sauce

1 tbsp (15 ml) honey

1 tbsp (15 ml) medium-dry or dry sherry, optional

1 ½ tsp (8 ml) cold-pressed or toasted sesame oil

1 tbsp (10 g) minced fresh ginger

4 cloves garlic, minced

¼ tsp crushed red pepper flakes

3 tbsp (24 g) cornstarch plus 3 tbsp (45 ml) water

1 ½ cups (167 g) roasted unsalted whole cashews, plus more for serving

Hot cooked rice, for serving

Place the chicken cubes in a large slow cooker. In a medium bowl, whisk together the chicken broth, oyster sauce, soy sauce, honey, sherry, sesame oil, ginger, garlic and crushed red pepper flakes. Pour the sauce over the chicken and stir until the chicken is evenly coated. Cover the slow cooker and cook on low for 2 ½ to 5 hours, until the chicken is cooked through and tender but not dry or falling apart—keep in mind that chicken breasts cook quicker than chicken thighs.

In a small bowl, mix the cornstarch and the water until smooth. Gently stir the cornstarch slurry into the slow cooker, breaking up any chicken pieces that are stuck together. Add the cashews. Cover the slow cooker and cook on high for 15 to 30 minutes, until the sauce has thickened. Serve over the rice and garnish with additional cashews, if desired.

# JAMBALAYA

If you think you can handle the heat, jambalaya is a rice-based recipe with several key ingredients in common with Spanish paella—but its flavors and spice level result in a decidedly different dish! This rendition incorporates the "holy trinity" of Louisiana cuisine: onions, celery and bell pepper. But thanks to the inclusion of tomatoes, it leans more toward a Creole influence as opposed to a Cajun one.

YIELD: 6 TO 8 SERVINGS

1 ½ lb (680 g) bone-in chicken thighs, skin removed and trimmed

12 oz (340 g) andouille sausage, cut into ¼-inch (6-mm) thick slices

½ medium yellow onion, finely chopped

½ medium green bell pepper, seeded and finely chopped

2 medium stalks celery, finely chopped

4 cloves garlic, minced

1 (14.5-oz [411-g]) can fire-roasted diced tomatoes

1 tbsp (15 ml) Worcestershire sauce

1 tbsp (12 g) House Seasoning (page 193)

1 tbsp (12 g) Creole seasoning (such as Tony Chachere's brand)

1 tbsp (3 g) dried thyme

1 tsp (1 g) dried oregano

2 dried bay leaves

2 cups (480 ml) low-sodium chicken broth

1 cup (211 g) uncooked long-grain white rice

½ lb (227 g) medium raw shrimp, peeled and deveined

Salt and freshly ground black pepper, to taste

Cayenne pepper, to taste, optional

Combine the chicken thighs, andouille sausage, onion, bell pepper, celery, garlic, diced tomatoes, Worcestershire sauce, House Seasoning, Creole seasoning, thyme, oregano, bay leaves and chicken broth in a large slow cooker. Cover the slow cooker and cook on low for 6 to 8 hours, or on high for 3 to 4 hours, until the chicken is cooked through.

Discard the bay leaves, transfer the chicken to a plate and stir the rice into the slow cooker. Cover the slow cooker and cook on high for 30 minutes or until the rice is done, watching closely, stirring halfway through, and adding a splash more water or broth *only* if all of the liquid gets soaked up too soon and the rice is about to start burning.

While the rice is cooking, pull the chicken meat off the bones and keep it warm. Bring a large saucepan of lightly salted water to a boil over high heat. Add the shrimp, reduce the heat to a simmer and cook, uncovered, for 1 to 3 minutes, until the shrimp turn pink and opaque. Drain the shrimp and stir them and the chicken into the slow cooker as soon as the rice is done cooking. Turn off the slow cooker, adjust the seasonings with the salt, pepper and cayenne pepper (if using) to taste and serve immediately.

# MARINATED PORK CHOPS AND POTATOES

Cooking pork chops in the slow cooker can be tricky since pork chops, like chicken breasts, are prone to drying out quickly. The secret is to buy the right *kind* of pork chop, and to be honest, it's not always easy to find. So if you don't see blade-cut pork chops in the meat case, ask your butcher to cut some for you, at least 1-inch (2.5-cm) thick. These chops are fattier, coming from near the shoulder of the pig, so they hold up better in the slow cooker.

The marinating in this recipe ensures flavorful chops, but it's up to you as to whether you'd like them to turn out juicy and medium (use a thermometer to ensure that you've reached a safe internal temperature) or tender and well done. Keep in mind that if you go for juicy chops with a short cooking time, your potatoes may not be completely tender in that amount of time. So be sure to slice them as thinly as possible to begin with, and if they're still a little too firm when the pork chops are done, return the potatoes to the slow cooker with a splash of broth, cover the slow cooker and cook the potatoes on high while you make the gravy and the pork chops rest.

YIELD: 4 SERVINGS

4 (1-inch [2.5-cm]) thick bone-in, blade-cut pork chops (about 2 to 2 ½ lb [910 g to 1.1 kg] total)

½ cup (120 ml) extra-virgin olive oil

¼ cup (60 ml) low-sodium soy sauce

2 tbsp (30 ml) honey

6 cloves garlic, minced

3 tbsp (9 g) Italian Seasoning (page 193), plus more for potatoes

1 ½ lb (680 g) red potatoes, cut into ⅛- to ¼-inch (3- to 6-mm) thick slices

House Seasoning (page 193), to taste

Freshly ground black pepper, to taste

½ cup (120 ml) low-sodium chicken broth, plus more for gravy

1 ½ tbsp (12 g) cornstarch plus 2 tbsp (30 ml) water

Pierce the pork chops all over with a fork. Combine the olive oil, soy sauce, honey, garlic and Italian Seasoning in a gallon (3.8-L)-size plastic zip-top bag. Add the pork chops, turn and squeeze the bag to coat all of the chops, and place the bag in a baking dish to marinate overnight (or at least 8 hours).

Layer the potatoes in a large slow cooker, lightly sprinkling them with the Italian Seasoning, House Seasoning and pepper. Remove the pork chops from the marinade and arrange them on top of the potatoes, overlapping but not placing them directly on top of one another. Pour the chicken broth into the bottom of the slow cooker.

For medium pork chops that are juicy, cover the slow cooker and cook on low for 2 to 4 hours, until a thermometer inserted in the center registers 145°F (63°C). For well-done pork chops that are fall-off-the-bone tender, cook on low for 6 to 8 hours, or until a thermometer registers 160°F (71°C).

Transfer the pork chops and potatoes to a platter, and tent them with foil to keep them warm. In a small bowl, mix the cornstarch and the water until smooth and set aside. Strain the juices from the slow cooker into a measuring cup and add enough chicken broth to measure 1 cup (240 ml). Pour the mixture into a medium saucepan and bring it to a boil over medium-high heat. Whisk the gravy continuously while slowly pouring in the cornstarch slurry. Reduce the heat to a simmer and cook for 1 to 2 minutes, stirring constantly, until the gravy has thickened. Serve the gravy over the pork chops and potatoes.

# SHEPHERD'S PIE

In the past, I've always made my Shepherd's Pie using ground beef that's been cooked in a skillet. But after adapting my tried and true recipe to the slow cooker, I'm thrilled with how this stew-like variation turned out! It's homey and comforting, loaded with satisfying chunks of beef and the rainbow of usual veggies in a thick, rich gravy.

YIELD: 6 TO 8 SERVINGS

1 ½ lb (680 g) boneless beef chuck roast, trimmed and cut into 1-inch (2.5-cm) cubes

3 cloves garlic, minced

4 medium carrots, peeled and cut into ¼-inch (6-mm) slices

8 oz (227 g) white mushrooms, cleaned and roughly chopped

1 ½ cups (217 g) frozen corn, thawed

¾ cup (180 ml) low-sodium beef broth

6 tbsp (100 g) tomato paste

2 tsp (10 ml) Worcestershire sauce

1 tsp (1 g) dried oregano

1 ½ tbsp (18 g) House Seasoning (page 193)

3 tbsp (24 g) all-purpose flour

1 ½ cups (240 g) frozen peas, thawed

Salt and freshly ground black pepper, to taste

1 ½ cups (6 oz [170 g]) shredded cheddar cheese

5 to 6 cups (1.1 to 1.3 kg) Mashed Potatoes (recipe follows)

MASHED POTATOES

2 ½ lb (1.1 kg) russet potatoes, peeled and cut into 2-inch (5-cm) pieces

1 tsp (6 g) salt

1 cup (240 ml) milk, warmed

6 tbsp (85 g) butter, melted

Salt and freshly ground black pepper, to taste

Place the beef cubes in a large slow cooker. Top with the garlic, carrots, mushrooms and corn. In a medium bowl, whisk together the beef broth, tomato paste, Worcestershire sauce, oregano and House Seasoning. Pour the broth mixture over the contents of the slow cooker and stir to combine. Cover the slow cooker and cook on low for 7 to 9 hours, or on high for 3 ½ to 4 ½ hours, until the beef is tender.

To make the mashed potatoes, place the potatoes in a large saucepan and cover them with 2 inches (5 cm) of water. Bring the potatoes to a boil over high heat and stir in the salt. Reduce the heat and simmer until the potatoes are tender when stabbed with a fork (start checking them at 15 minutes).

Drain the potatoes, and return them to the pot. Add the milk, butter, salt and pepper to taste. Gently mash the potatoes with a handheld potato masher.

Use a large spoon to skim any fat from the surface of the beef and veggie mixture in the slow cooker. In a small bowl, mix the flour and 6 tablespoons (90 ml) water until smooth, then slowly stir the mixture into the slow cooker. Add the peas. Adjust the seasonings to taste with salt and pepper. Mix the cheddar into the Mashed Potatoes and spread in an even layer over the top of the beef and vegetables. Cover the slow cooker and cook on high for 15 to 30 minutes, until the gravy has thickened and the Mashed Potatoes are heated through.

# BARBECUE-SAUCE CHICKEN THIGHS

This one is sure to become a family favorite, folks. Bone-in chicken thighs turn tender and succulent as they slow cook in a sweet and savory, homemade barbecue sauce. I prefer leaving the skin on when making this recipe so that once the chicken thighs are finished cooking, I can pop them under the broiler to crisp up. But you can also pull the skin off your chicken thighs before putting them in the slow cooker and skip the broiling step. Your chicken is guaranteed to be delicious either way!

YIELD: 4 TO 6 SERVINGS

8 bone-in, skin-on chicken thighs, trimmed (about 3 lb [1.4 kg] total)

½ cup (125 g) all-natural ketchup

½ cup (126 g) tomato sauce

4 tbsp (67 g) tomato paste

¼ cup (60 ml) honey

3 tbsp (45 ml) molasses

3 tbsp (45 ml) apple cider vinegar

1 tsp (5 ml) Worcestershire sauce

2 cloves garlic, minced

1 tbsp (12 g) House Seasoning (page 193)

¼ tsp smoked paprika

¼ tsp chili powder

⅛ tsp ground cumin

Freshly ground black pepper, to taste

Pinch cayenne pepper, optional

Place the chicken thighs in a large slow cooker. In a medium bowl, combine the ketchup, tomato sauce, tomato paste, honey, molasses, apple cider vinegar, Worcestershire sauce, garlic, House Seasoning, smoked paprika, chili powder, cumin, pepper and cayenne pepper (if using). Pour the sauce over the chicken thighs, then cover the slow cooker and cook on low for 4 to 6 hours, until the chicken is tender and cooked through.

Position an oven rack 8 to 10 inches (20 to 25 cm) below the heating element and preheat the broiler. Line a large, rimmed baking sheet with foil and transfer the chicken to the baking sheet, skin-side up. Skim the fat from the surface of the barbecue sauce in the slow cooker, then spoon a thin layer of sauce over the chicken thighs until they're evenly covered. Broil the chicken thighs for 5 to 10 minutes, watching them carefully, until they are crispy and browned. Turn the pan halfway through if it looks like the chicken is not browning evenly. Serve the broiled chicken thighs with the remaining barbecue sauce on the side.

# CHEESEBURGER MACARONI

As a child of the '80s, I loved dinners originating from that smiling, slightly creepy, white glove–adorned box. And as a college student. And as a young adult. But when I had kids of my own, it suddenly occurred to me to check the ingredients contained in my beloved pasta and powdered sauce mix goodness, and . . . *yikes.* So I devised a delicious homemade version and all was right in the world again. This slow cooker adaptation of *that* recipe is super easy and totally yummy. While it may seem like a strange addition, the honey is included to replicate the sugar in the original boxed mix, but it also helps combat acidity from the diced tomatoes. Also, like the original, this recipe is very mild. But if you prefer a little spice, that's easy to remedy by throwing in a can of diced green chiles or adding some cayenne or hot sauce. Ground turkey would work just fine in this dish, and you *always* have my permission to up the amount of cheese should you so wish.

Yep, this one is a big hit at our house. I hope your crew loves it, too!

YIELD: 8 TO 10 SERVINGS

2 lb (910 g) lean ground beef (90 percent lean)

4 cloves garlic, minced

1 tbsp (12 g) House Seasoning (page 193)

2 tsp (5 g) chili powder

2 tsp (4 g) paprika

1 tsp (5 ml) honey

2 (14.5-oz [411-g]) cans fire-roasted diced tomatoes

4 cups (1 L) low-sodium beef broth, divided

2 cups (224 g) small elbow macaroni

3 cups (12 oz [340 g]) shredded sharp cheddar cheese

Salt and freshly ground black pepper, to taste

In a large saucepan over medium-high heat, brown the ground beef until it is cooked through, stirring in the garlic during the last 1 to 2 minutes. Drain the grease. Stir in the House Seasoning, chili powder, paprika and honey. Allow the ground beef mixture to cool for a few minutes before transferring it to a large slow cooker. Pour the diced tomatoes and 2 cups (480 ml) of the beef broth over the top of the ground beef, stirring to combine. Cover the slow cooker and cook on low for 4 to 6 hours, or on high for 2 ½ to 3 ½ hours.

Stir in the remaining 2 cups (480 ml) beef broth and the macaroni. Cover the slow cooker and cook on high for 30 to 45 minutes, until the pasta is al dente, stirring halfway through and watching the liquid level carefully. Add a bit more beef broth or water toward the end *only* if necessary. Add the cheddar, stirring until it has melted, adjust the seasoning to taste with salt and pepper and serve hot.

# RED BEANS AND RICE

A beloved Louisiana institution, every family has their own special way of making red beans and rice. Not traditionally as spicy as other Creole cuisine, it's still easy to adjust the heat of this dish by switching out the sausage, adding more Creole seasoning to the slow cooker or simply offering hot sauce at the table so that individual portions can be tweaked. It *is* important to boil red kidney beans for ten minutes before adding them to the slow cooker for food safety reasons, but smashing some of the cooked beans before serving is optional.

YIELD: 6 SERVINGS

1 lb (455 g) dried red kidney beans, picked over, rinsed and drained

6 cups (1.4 L) low-sodium chicken broth

8 oz (225 g) smoked sausage (for mild) or andouille sausage (for spicy), cut into ¼-inch (6-mm) thick slices

1 medium yellow onion, finely chopped

½ medium green bell pepper, seeded and finely chopped

2 medium stalks celery, finely chopped

6 cloves garlic, minced

3 dried bay leaves

1 tbsp (2 g) dried parsley

1 tsp (4 g) Creole seasoning (such as Tony Chachere's brand), plus more to taste

½ tsp dried thyme

½ tsp dried basil

½ tsp smoked paprika

½ tsp salt, plus more to taste

Freshly ground black pepper, to taste

Cayenne pepper, to taste

Hot sauce (such as Tabasco, Louisiana or Crystal brands), to taste

Warm cooked rice, for serving

Place the kidney beans in a medium saucepan and cover them with 2 inches (5 cm) of water. Bring the beans to a boil over high heat and boil for 10 minutes. Drain the water and transfer the kidney beans to a large slow cooker. Add the chicken broth, smoked or andouille sausage, onion, bell pepper, celery, garlic, bay leaves, parsley, Creole seasoning, thyme, basil and smoked paprika. Cover the slow cooker and cook on low for 8 to 10 hours, or on high for 4 to 5 hours, until the beans are tender.

Using a slotted spoon, scoop out 2 cups (354 g) of the cooked beans (avoiding the sausage). Smash the beans with a fork until they are smooth and stir them back into the slow cooker. Alternatively, use a blender or small food processor to purée the beans. Stir in the salt and a few grinds of pepper, then taste and add more salt and pepper, if desired. If extra heat is preferred, stir in additional Creole seasoning (just remember that there's salt in there, too), cayenne pepper or hot sauce, to taste. Cover the slow cooker and cook for 10 minutes, until the beans are heated through. Discard the bay leaves and serve the beans over the rice with hot sauce, if desired.

## Samantha's Tip

An important fact about cooking dried kidney beans in the slow cooker is that raw or undercooked kidney beans, especially red kidney beans, contain a high level of a naturally occurring toxin called phytohaemagglutinin that can cause severe intestinal distress (a.k.a. food poisoning). Therefore, it is always critical to bring dried kidney beans to a rolling boil for 10 minutes in order to remove this toxin and make them safe to eat. Since some slow cookers run cooler than others, the only way to guarantee safe kidney beans is to boil them on the stove before draining and transferring the beans to the slow cooker.

# INDIAN BUTTER CHICKEN

Sometimes it's fun to surprise family or friends with an *exotic* dinner that came out of the slow cooker. People will likely have a hard time believing that this spin on a popular restaurant-style Indian dish was prepared in an all-American slow cooker!

Ironically, despite is name, butter chicken actually involves very little butter. It *does* typically contain heavy cream, but I've lightened that up a bit in this recipe by subbing Greek yogurt and half-and-half instead. So the next time you're in the mood for something different, let the warm spices and creamy sauce of this chicken transport you to a faraway land!

YIELD: 4 TO 6 SERVINGS

2 lb (910 g) boneless, skinless chicken breasts or thighs, trimmed and cut into 1 ½-inch (4-cm) cubes

4 tbsp (67 g) tomato paste

4 cloves garlic, minced

1 tbsp (10 g) minced fresh ginger

1 tbsp (15 g) Thai red curry paste

1 tbsp (7 g) garam masala

2 tsp (5 g) curry powder

1 tsp (2 g) ground cumin

1 tsp (1 g) ground cardamom

½ tsp salt, plus more to taste

¼ tsp ground turmeric

¼ tsp cayenne pepper, optional, plus more to taste

1 tbsp (15 ml) water

¾ cup (170 g) full-fat Greek yogurt

½ cup (120 ml) half-and-half

1 tbsp (14 g) butter

Hot cooked basmati rice (or other long-grain), for serving

Chopped fresh cilantro, optional, for garnishing

Naan bread, for serving

Place the chicken cubes in a large slow cooker. In a medium bowl, whisk together the tomato paste, garlic, ginger, curry paste, garam masala, curry powder, cumin, cardamom, salt, turmeric, cayenne pepper (if using) and water until smooth. Pour the sauce over the chicken and stir until the chicken is evenly coated. Cover the slow cooker and cook on low for 2 ½ to 5 hours, until the chicken is cooked through and tender but not dry or falling apart—keep in mind that chicken breasts cook quicker than chicken thighs.

Add the Greek yogurt to a medium bowl and mix in the half-and-half. Temper the yogurt mixture, to prevent curdling, by spooning some warm sauce from the slow cooker into the yogurt mixture and stirring well. Add more sauce and a few pieces of chicken and stir again. Repeat this process several times to gradually bring up the temperature of the yogurt mixture. Once the yogurt-chicken mixture is warm, pour it back into the slow cooker over the remaining chicken, and gently stir to combine. Season with additional salt to taste, then add the butter. Cover the slow cooker and cook for 5 to 10 minutes, until the butter is melted and the chicken and sauce are heated through. Stir and serve over the rice, garnish with the cilantro and serve the naan bread on the side.

# HUNGARIAN GOULASH

There are countless variations of goulash out there, originating from an array of different countries, but this one attempts to honor the dish as it was first conceived in Hungary. If you can track down sweet Hungarian paprika, fabulous! It definitely adds authentic flavor to this recipe. But if not, regular ol' paprika will work fine (just make sure it's not hot or smoked). When I was growing up, my German mother always served Hungarian goulash over hot cooked egg noodles, so that part may not be historically accurate, but I can assure you it's tasty!

YIELD: 6 TO 8 SERVINGS

1 ½ lb (680 g) boneless beef chuck roast, trimmed and cut into 1-inch (2.5-cm) cubes

1 lb (454 g) red or yellow potatoes, peeled and cut into 1-inch (2.5-cm) cubes

2 medium carrots, peeled and cut into ½-inch (13-mm) slices

1 medium yellow onion, finely chopped

1 medium red bell pepper, seeded and finely chopped

4 cloves garlic, minced

3 tbsp (21 g) sweet Hungarian paprika or regular paprika

1 tbsp (12 g) House Seasoning (page 193)

2 tsp (1 g) dried marjoram

¼ tsp caraway seeds

3 cups (720 ml) low-sodium beef broth

1 tbsp (17 g) tomato paste

1 dried bay leaf

3 tbsp (24 g) all-purpose flour plus 6 tbsp (90 ml) water

Salt and freshly ground black pepper, to taste

Hot cooked egg noodles, for serving

Sour cream, for serving, optional

Combine the beef cubes, potatoes, carrots, onion, bell pepper, garlic, paprika, House Seasoning, marjoram, caraway seeds, beef broth and tomato paste in a large slow cooker. Stir well to combine and add the bay leaf. Cover the slow cooker and cook on low for 7 to 9 hours, or on high for 3 ½ to 4 ½ hours, until the beef is tender.

Discard the bay leaf and use a large spoon to skim any fat from the surface of the goulash. In a small bowl, mix the flour and the water until smooth, then slowly stir the mixture into the slow cooker. Cover the slow cooker and cook on high for 15 to 30 minutes, until the gravy has thickened. Adjust the seasonings to taste with salt and pepper. Serve the goulash over the hot cooked egg noodles with a dollop of the sour cream (if using).

# PAELLA

If you're craving the flavors of paella without all of the work, give this simple slow cooker version a whirl! In addition to chicken and shrimp, this dish features Spanish chorizo, a dried, cured sausage. Spanish chorizo is often found near the deli section with the other dried sausages, and it's different than Mexican chorizo, which is sold uncooked in casings and has to be crumbled and browned in a pan. Finally, while paella is traditionally flavored with saffron, these highly prized Crocus flower stigmas are rather pricey, so feel free to leave them out.

YIELD: 8 SERVINGS

1 ½ lb (680 g) boneless, skinless chicken thighs, cut into 1-inch (2.5-cm) cubes

6 oz (170 g) dried Spanish chorizo, cut into ¼-inch (6-mm) thick slices

½ medium yellow or Spanish onion, finely chopped

6 cloves garlic, minced

1 (14.5-oz [411-g]) can diced tomatoes

1 tbsp (12 g) House Seasoning (page 193)

2 tsp (4 g) paprika

½ tsp smoked paprika

½ tsp dried oregano

¼ to ½ tsp crushed red pepper flakes

¼ tsp saffron threads, optional

2 dried bay leaves

2 tsp (10 ml) freshly squeezed lemon juice

2 cups (480 ml) low-sodium chicken broth

½ cup (120 ml) dry white wine (such as Chardonnay or Pinot Grigio)

1 ½ cups (316 g) uncooked short-grain white rice (preferably arborio rice)

½ lb (225 g) medium raw shrimp, peeled and deveined

1 ½ cups (201 g) frozen peas, thawed

½ cup (20 g) chopped fresh parsley

Salt and freshly ground black pepper, to taste

Lemon wedges, for serving

Combine the chicken cubes, chorizo sausage, onion, garlic, diced tomatoes, House Seasoning, paprika, smoked paprika, oregano, crushed red pepper flakes, saffron, bay leaves, lemon juice, chicken broth and white wine in a large slow cooker. Cover the slow cooker and cook on low for 4 to 6 hours, or on high for 2 to 3 hours, until the chicken is cooked through.

Discard the bay leaves and stir the rice into the slow cooker. Cover the slow cooker and cook on high for 30 minutes or until the rice is done, watching closely, stirring halfway through, and adding a splash more water or broth *only* if all of the liquid gets soaked up too soon and the rice is about to start burning.

While the rice is cooking, bring a large saucepan of lightly salted water to a boil over high heat. Add the shrimp, reduce the heat to a simmer and cook, uncovered, for 1 to 3 minutes, until the shrimp turn pink and opaque. Drain the shrimp and stir them into the slow cooker as soon as the rice is done cooking. Add the peas and parsley. Turn off the slow cooker, adjust the seasoning with salt and pepper to taste, and serve immediately with the lemon wedges.

# COMFORTING MAIN DISHES

## Thirteen Decidedly Delicious Dinner Ideas

Hope you're hungry, because this chapter is filled to the brim with tasty dinner ideas and classic recipes that have been given a whole new twist!

Sometimes it's surprising to learn exactly what can be cooked in the slow cooker. Need enough Italian food for a crowd? Whip up a big batch of Cheesy Spinach Lasagna (page 64). Do ribs sound good but you don't exactly feel like brushing the snow off the grill? Honey-Garlic Baby Back Ribs (page 63) turn out fall-apart tender after hours in the slow cooker. And if you're on the hunt for a dinner party–worthy entrée, Bacon-Wrapped Peach Jalapeño Pork Loin (page 52) is both delectable *and* impressive.

Other times, it's nice to come home to a creative spin on a familiar family favorite. Messy sandwiches and meatloaf collide in Sloppy Joe Meatloaf (page 72). Homemade white sauce skips the fettuccine in Chicken Alfredo Tortellini (page 71). And chuck roast goes south of the border via Mexican Pot Roast with Borracho Beans (page 60).

The next time you're stuck in a rut for a dinner idea, give one of these comforting main dishes a try. All of them are sure to leave your taste buds happy!

# BACON-WRAPPED PEACH JALAPEÑO PORK LOIN

This is probably one of the fanciest-looking meals that you'll ever pull out of your slow cooker, but the preparation is deceptively simple! Bacon-wrapped pork loin glazed with a sweet and spicy peach-jalapeño sauce is a dinner that your family and guests won't soon forget. I include the jalapeño seeds when I make the glaze, because I want it to be a bit spicy, and I find that one large minced jalapeño is the right level of heat for my family—warm but not over the top. Add more or less to taste, but keep in mind that the jalapeños will become milder as they cook, so if you taste your glaze as you initially prepare it, it can stand to be a tad hotter than you actually want it to turn out. Make sure to use regular bacon that's not too thin or too thick, and you may need slightly more or less of it depending upon the width and length of your pork loin (see my pork loin recommendations on page 16). As always, be sure to watch your pork loin closely once you pop it under the broiler, as the bacon can go from perfectly crisp to completely burned in a matter of seconds.

YIELD: 6 TO 8 SERVINGS

3 lb (1.4 kg) pork loin

Salt and freshly ground black pepper, to taste

6 slices bacon, cut in half (about 6 oz [170 g] total)

¼ cup (60 ml) low-sodium chicken broth or water

2 cups (20 oz [570 g]) peach preserves

1 to 2 medium jalapeños, minced

1 ½ tbsp (23 ml) soy sauce

1 ½ tbsp (23 g) Dijon mustard

Trim as much of the fat cap as possible from the top of the pork loin. Very generously season both sides of the pork loin with salt and pepper and rub them into the meat. Place the pork loin (fat-side up, if any fat remains) in the bottom of a large oval slow cooker. Starting at one end of the pork, lay the half-strips of bacon over the top, crosswise and overlapping slightly until the entire pork loin is covered. Pour the chicken broth or water into the bottom of the slow cooker.

Prepare the glaze by combining the peach preserves, jalapeños, soy sauce and Dijon mustard in a medium bowl. Transfer 1 ½ cups (360 ml) of the glaze to a small bowl. Cover the bowl and refrigerate it. Spoon the remaining glaze over the bacon-covered pork loin, trying to keep most of it on top with just a thin layer going down the sides—you don't want all of the glaze running off as soon as the heat hits the pork.

Cover the slow cooker and cook on low for 2 to 4 hours, until the center of the pork loin just reaches 145°F (63°C) on an instant-read thermometer. Position an oven rack 6 inches (15 cm) below the heating element and preheat the broiler. Line a large, rimmed baking sheet with foil and transfer the pork loin to the baking sheet.

Broil the pork loin for a few minutes, until the bacon is crispy and browned, watching carefully the entire time. Remove the pork loin from the oven, spoon a thick layer of the reserved peach-jalapeño glaze over the pork, and broil for 1 to 2 more minutes, until the glaze is bubbly.

Transfer the pork loin to a cutting board, tent it with foil and allow it to rest for 15 minutes. While the pork rests, transfer the remaining peach-jalapeño glaze to a small saucepan over medium heat. Cook the glaze, stirring occasionally, for about 5 minutes, until it is bubbly and the jalapeños are softened. Cut the pork loin into ½-inch (13-mm) thick slices and serve drizzled with the warm glaze.

# SALISBURY STEAK MEATBALLS

In this creative spin on a classic, Salisbury Steak patties are miniaturized into meatballs and cooked in their traditional onion- and mushroom-laden gravy. The result is a homey, satisfying supper that's tasty on its own but even better over Mashed Potatoes (page 37). Hey, at least those frozen dinners of yore got that part right!

YIELD: 6 TO 8 SERVINGS

1 medium yellow onion, cut into ¼-inch (6-mm) slices

8 oz (227 g) white mushrooms, cleaned and cut into ⅛- to ¼-inch (3- to 6-mm) thick slices

STEAK MEATBALLS

2 lb (910 g) lean ground beef (90 percent lean)

1 cup (120 g) unseasoned dried or fresh breadcrumbs

½ cup (120 ml) whole milk

1 tbsp (15 ml) Worcestershire sauce

1 tbsp (2 g) dried parsley

1 tbsp (12 g) House Seasoning (page 193)

1 tsp (2 g) mustard powder

GRAVY

2 cups (480 ml) low-sodium beef broth

1 tbsp (17 g) tomato paste

1 tbsp (15 ml) Worcestershire sauce

1 tsp (2 g) mustard powder

2 tsp (8 g) House Seasoning (page 193)

3 tbsp (24 g) cornstarch plus 3 tbsp (45 ml) cool water

Salt and freshly ground black pepper, to taste

Hot Mashed Potatoes (page 37) or cooked egg noodles, for serving

Place the onions and mushrooms in the bottom of a large slow cooker. In a large bowl, thoroughly combine the ground beef, breadcrumbs, milk, Worcestershire sauce, parsley, House Seasoning and mustard powder, and form into 24 equally sized meatballs (see Samantha's Tip for the Swedish Meatballs on page 29). Arrange a layer of meatballs over the onions and mushrooms in the slow cooker, and add the remaining meatballs in a second layer on top.

In another large bowl, whisk together the beef broth, tomato paste, Worcestershire sauce, mustard powder and House Seasoning. Evenly pour this mixture over the meatballs in the slow cooker. Cover the slow cooker and cook on low for 8 hours, or on high for 4 hours, until the meatballs are cooked through yet still tender. Homemade meatballs cooked in the slow cooker may still look slightly pink in the center even after they are fully cooked, but they are safe to eat once they have reached an internal temperature of 160°F (71°C)—see page 14 for a more detailed explanation.

Use a slotted spoon to transfer the meatballs, onions and mushrooms to a platter. Cover the platter to keep them warm. Skim the fat from the surface of the gravy in the slow cooker. In a small bowl, mix the cornstarch and the water until smooth, and whisk the cornstarch slurry into the slow cooker. Add the meatballs, onions and mushrooms back to slow cooker and stir well. Adjust the seasoning of the gravy with salt and pepper to taste. Cover the slow cooker and cook on high for 30 minutes and serve the meatballs hot over the Mashed Potatoes or noodles.

# CHICKEN STROGANOFF

Slow cooker stroganoff traditionally relies on cream of mushroom soup for its creaminess. But not this version, which, in addition to nixing the processed ingredients, puts a unique spin on a classic by exchanging chicken for beef. Tender chunks of chicken and fresh mushrooms are flavored with Worcestershire, Dijon and a splash of white wine, with both sour cream and cream cheese stirred in at the end for that signature creamy sauce. A pop of freshness from minced parsley and a homey bed of egg noodles are all you need to complete this comforting dish.

YIELD: 4 TO 6 SERVINGS

2 lb (910 g) boneless, skinless chicken breasts or thighs, trimmed and cut into 1-inch (2.5-cm) cubes

12 oz (340 g) white mushrooms, cleaned and cut into ⅛- to ¼-inch (3- to 6-mm) thick slices

4 cloves garlic, minced

1 ½ cups (360 ml) low-sodium chicken broth

2 tbsp (30 ml) dry white wine (such as Chardonnay or Pinot Grigio), optional

1 tbsp (15 ml) Worcestershire sauce

1 tbsp (15 g) Dijon mustard

1 tbsp (12 g) House Seasoning (page 193)

½ tsp dried thyme

6 tbsp (45 g) all-purpose flour

1 dried bay leaf

4 oz (112 g) cream cheese, cubed and at room temperature

8 oz (227 g) sour cream

½ cup (25 g) minced fresh parsley, plus more for garnishing

Salt and freshly ground black pepper, to taste

Hot cooked egg noodles, for serving

Combine the chicken cubes, mushrooms and garlic in a large slow cooker. In a medium bowl, whisk together the chicken broth, white wine (if using), Worcestershire sauce, Dijon mustard, House Seasoning, thyme and flour until smooth. Pour the mixture into the slow cooker and stir to coat the chicken. Add the bay leaf, cover the slow cooker and cook on low for 2 ½ to 5 hours, until the chicken is cooked through and tender but not dry or falling apart—keep in mind that chicken breasts cook quicker than chicken thighs.

Gently stir the chicken and mushrooms, scatter the cubed cream cheese on top of the chicken and mushroom mixture, and replace the lid. After 10 minutes, stir the warm cream cheese into the sauce, breaking it up with the back of a spoon to incorporate it.

Add the sour cream to a medium bowl and temper it, to prevent curdling, by spooning some warm sauce from the slow cooker into the sour cream and stirring well. Add more sauce to the sour cream and stir again. Repeat this process several times to gradually bring up the temperature of the sour cream. Once the sour cream is warm, pour it back into the slow cooker along with the parsley, and stir until all the ingredients are thoroughly combined. Adjust the seasoning with salt and pepper to taste, then cover the slow cooker and cook for 5 to 10 minutes, until the sauce is heated through. Stir the stroganoff well before serving it over hot cooked egg noodles with a garnish of minced fresh parsley.

# STACKED SANTA FE CHICKEN ENCHILADAS

Enchiladas in the slow cooker? *Inconceivable!* But, happily, it's true. These aren't your traditional rolled chicken enchiladas, however. Rather, they're stacked for ease of assembly and each serving is topped with a fried egg, New Mexico–style, which is entirely optional but totally delicious. The meat from a rotisserie chicken provides about the right amount for this recipe, but you can use leftover chicken or turkey, or—if all else fails—you can poach 2 pounds ([907 g], or about four average-size) boneless, skinless chicken breasts and chop those up. As for the type of tortillas to use, corn tortillas can disintegrate and flour tortillas can become gummy, so *mixed* corn and wheat flour tortillas are ideal. That being said, straight corn or straight flour tortillas will definitely work if that's all you can find—just choose whichever variety is your favorite and consider cooking this recipe for a slightly shorter length of time to help maintain the integrity of the tortillas.

YIELD: 6 TO 8 SERVINGS

4 cups (560 g) diced cooked chicken

4 cloves garlic

1 (14.5-oz [411-g]) can fire-roasted diced tomatoes, drained

2 tbsp (33 g) tomato paste

1 cup (240 ml) low-sodium chicken broth

3 tbsp (24 g) chili powder

2 tbsp (16 g) all-purpose flour

1 tbsp (12 g) House Seasoning (page 193)

2 tsp (5 g) ground cumin

1 tsp (5 ml) honey

½ tsp dried Mexican oregano

1 chipotle pepper in adobo sauce, seeded

9 (6-inch [15-cm]) corn and wheat flour blend tortillas (such as Mission brand Mission Artisan Corn and Wheat Blend or H-E-B brand H-E-B Mixla Corn and Flour Blend)

2 cups (8 oz [230 g]) shredded Monterey Jack cheese

1 fried egg per person, optional

Pico de gallo, for serving

Place the diced chicken in a large bowl. In a blender or food processor, pulse the garlic until it is minced. Add the drained diced tomatoes, tomato paste, chicken broth, chili powder, flour, House Seasoning, cumin, honey, Mexican oregano and chipotle pepper and purée until smooth. Pour the sauce over the chicken in the bowl and mix until well combined.

Generously coat a large oval slow cooker with cooking spray. Arrange 3 tortillas in the bottom of the slow cooker, tearing a tortilla into pieces (if necessary) in order to cover most of the open spaces. Layer with ⅓ of the chicken mixture and ⅓ of the Monterey Jack. Repeat this process twice, for 2 more layers of tortillas, chicken and Monterey Jack.

Cover the slow cooker and cook on low for 2 ½ to 4 hours, until the enchiladas are heated through, occasionally checking the edges of the tortillas to make sure that they aren't starting to burn. Turn off the slow cooker and allow the enchiladas to rest for 30 minutes before cutting them into wedges and serving. Top each serving with a fried egg (if using) and serve the pico de gallo on the side.

# MEXICAN POT ROAST WITH BORRACHO BEANS

Give your regular ol' pot roast a south-of-the-border twist with this bold and zesty meal that's bursting with the flavors of chipotle, cilantro and lime. And as if that's not delicious enough, this recipe boasts a built-in side dish. The beef cooks in a pool of Mexican beer and spices atop a bed of pinto beans, simultaneously transforming them into "frijoles borrachos," which literally translates to "drunken beans" in Spanish. Add a side of cornbread to soak up the juices from the beans and you've got a satisfying supper that'll make you shout, "Olé!"

YIELD: 6 SERVINGS

1 cup (7 oz [200 g]) dried pinto beans, picked over, rinsed and drained

1 ½ cups (360 ml) low-sodium beef broth

1 (12-oz [355-ml]) bottle dark beer (see page 17 for recommendations)

2 dried bay leaves

3 ½ to 4 lb (1.6 to 1.8 kg) boneless beef chuck roast, trimmed

Salt and freshly ground black pepper, to taste

8 cloves garlic

¾ cup (30 g) packed fresh cilantro leaves

1 to 2 chipotle peppers in adobo sauce

1 to 2 tbsp (15 to 30 g) adobo sauce

3 tbsp (45 ml) freshly squeezed lime juice

1 ½ tbsp (25 g) tomato paste

1 ½ tbsp (10 g) ground cumin

1 tbsp (12 g) House Seasoning (page 193)

1 tbsp (8 g) chili powder

2 tsp (2 g) dried Mexican oregano

Cornbread, for serving

Place the beans in the bottom of a large slow cooker. Pour in the beef broth and beer. Stir to combine and add the bay leaves.

Generously season both sides of the roast with salt and pepper to taste, and lay the roast on top of the beans. In a blender or food processor, pulse the garlic and cilantro until they are minced. Add the chipotle peppers, adobo sauce, lime juice, tomato paste, cumin, House Seasoning, chili powder and Mexican oregano and pulse until smooth. Spread half of the garlic-cilantro mixture over the top of the roast. Carefully flip the roast over and spread the remaining garlic-cilantro mixture on the other side. Cover the slow cooker and cook on low for 8 to 10 hours, or on on high for 5 to 6 hours, until the roast and beans are tender.

Transfer the roast to a platter and use a large spoon to skim any excess fat from the surface of the cooking liquids. Discard the bay leaves. Serve the roast with a side of beans and cornbread to soak up the juices from the beans.

# HONEY-GARLIC BABY BACK RIBS

Ribs aren't just reserved for summertime barbecue season. Enjoy them any time of year, hot from the slow cooker! It may sound crazy, but after a dry-rubbed stint in the slow cooker, a glaze of homemade honey-garlic barbecue sauce and a quick turn under the broiler, these succulent ribs rival anything coming from the pit. It may take some experimentation with your particular slow cooker to determine the ideal cooking time for your ribs—too short and they won't be as tender as they could be, too long and the meat will fall straight off the bones when you try to lift them—but for me, it consistently ends up being around six and a half hours. Don't skimp on the sauce when basting—you want a nice, thick layer. And if you need to broil your ribs a bit longer to get them all sticky and caramelized (or shorter to prevent them from burning), that's perfectly fine. Just watch them closely, and they'll turn out fabulous!

YIELD: 6 TO 8 SERVINGS

2 (2 ½- to 3-lb [1.1- to 1.4-kg]) racks pork baby back ribs (5 to 6 lb [2.3 to 2.7 kg] total)

RIB RUB

3 tbsp (21 g) paprika

1 tbsp (7 g) smoked paprika

1 tbsp (10 g) garlic powder

1 tbsp (7 g) mustard powder

1 tbsp (7 g) ground ginger

1 tsp (6 g) salt

¼ tsp ground allspice

¼ tsp cayenne pepper

SAUCE

1 ½ cups (355 ml) honey

¾ cup (180 ml) reduced-sodium soy sauce

¾ cup (177 ml) all-natural ketchup

10 cloves garlic, minced

¼ tsp crushed red pepper flakes

Cut each rack of ribs in half. In a small bowl, prepare the spice rub by combining the paprika, smoked paprika, garlic powder, mustard powder, ginger, salt, allspice and cayenne pepper until well blended.  Rub the spice mixture all over both sides of each rack of ribs, coating them evenly.

Stand the ribs along the walls of a large oval slow cooker (with wide ends down and meaty sides facing the exterior). Cover the slow cooker and cook on low for 6 to 8 hours, until the ribs are tender.

While the ribs are cooking, prepare the sauce by combining the honey, soy sauce, ketchup, garlic and crushed red pepper flakes in a large saucepan over medium-high heat. Bring the mixture to a boil and then reduce to a simmer. Cook, stirring occasionally, for 15 minutes, until the sauce has thickened and reduced by about ⅓.

Position an oven rack 8 inches (20 cm) below the heating element and preheat the broiler. Line a large, rimmed baking sheet with heavy-duty aluminum foil. Use tongs and a metal spatula to transfer the ribs to the prepared baking sheet, meaty-side down. Spoon or brush the sauce over the ribs and broil them for 4 minutes. Carefully turn the ribs over, generously brush them with additional sauce and continue to broil for about 8 minutes, or until the ribs are browned and the sauce is caramelized, brushing with sauce once more about halfway through the cooking time.

Tent the ribs with foil and allow them to rest for 10 minutes before transferring them to a cutting board and slicing. Serve the ribs with the leftover sauce.

# CHEESY SPINACH LASAGNA

Slow cooker lasagna is a great way to feed a crowd while freeing up the oven. This yummy vegetarian version is layered with spinach-flecked ricotta, flavor-infused marinara sauce, masses of melty mozzarella and plenty of Parmesan. With no beef or sausage to precook, this lasagna is as easy as assembling the layers and going on your merry way for the next few hours. You'll know it's done when the noodles are just tender, so be sure to watch this recipe closely the first time you make it. And then? Prepare to be lauded with lasagna-loving cheers and accolades!

YIELD: 8 SERVINGS

3 (10-oz [283-g]) boxes frozen spinach, thawed and drained

1 (15-oz [425-g]) container ricotta cheese

1 egg

1 tsp (2 g) dried parsley

1 ¼ cups (140 g) freshly grated Parmesan cheese, divided

2 (24-oz [680-g]) jars marinara sauce (or about 6 cups [1.4 L] homemade sauce)

½ cup (120 ml) water

3 tbsp (50 g) tomato paste

1 tbsp (3 g) Italian Seasoning (page 193)

½ tsp garlic powder

¼ tsp crushed red pepper flakes

12 uncooked lasagna noodles (do not use no-boil noodles)

4 cups (16 oz [454 g]) shredded mozzarella cheese

Fresh basil chiffonade, for serving

In a large bowl, combine the spinach, ricotta, egg, parsley and ¾ cup (84 g) of the Parmesan until well blended and set aside. In another large bowl, combine the marinara sauce, water, tomato paste, Italian Seasoning, garlic powder and crushed red pepper flakes and set aside.

Spoon ½ cup (120 ml) of the sauce into the bottom of a large oval slow cooker and spread it into a thin layer. Place 3 lasagna noodles on top of the sauce, breaking a noodle into pieces (if necessary) in order to cover most of the blank spaces. Dollop ¼ of the spinach-ricotta mixture in small spoonfuls on top of the noodles and gently spread it into an even layer. Spread 1 ½ cups (360 ml) marinara sauce on top of the spinach-ricotta mixture. Sprinkle the top of this layer with 1 cup (114 g) of the shredded mozzarella and 2 tablespoons (22 g) of the remaining grated Parmesan.

Repeat these layers 3 more times, starting with the noodles and ending with the mozzarella and Parmesan topping. Cover the slow cooker and cook on low for 3 ½ to 4 hours, until the noodles are tender but not overcooked. Turn off the slow cooker and allow the lasagna to rest for 30 minutes before slicing and serving.

## Samantha's Tips

An easy way to drain frozen spinach is to thaw it completely, wrap it inside a clean kitchen towel, twist the ends and wring it out over the sink until completely dry. Alternatively, if you don't want a spinach-dyed towel, line a colander with 3 to 4 layers of paper towels extending up the sides, place the thawed spinach in the center, fold over the edges of the paper towels, and push and squeeze all of the water out through the bottom of the colander.

In order to use an equal amount of spinach-ricotta mixture for each layer of the lasagna, smooth the top of the spinach-ricotta mixture in the bowl and then use a butter knife to cut a straight line through the center from top to bottom, and then a second line through the center from side to side. This essentially divides the mixture into four equal parts, making it easy to scoop out ¼ of the mixture for each layer.

# SALSA VERDE PORK

This juicy, savory pork relies on the shortcut ingredient of store-bought salsa verde, a zesty green salsa brimming with tomatillos, hot peppers and cilantro. You will probably find several brands available in the Mexican food section of most grocery stores these days, but be sure to look for one with all-natural ingredients and no MSG. More green goodness is added to this dish in the form of diced green chiles, fresh jalapeños and fresh cilantro. My favorite way to eat this Salsa Verde Pork is with a copious amount of shredded pepper Jack cheese melted over the top, even more jalapeños and cilantro and a few slices of creamy avocado to cool things off. But it's also delicious to wrap the whole shebang in a warm flour tortilla.

YIELD: 6 TO 8 SERVINGS

3 ½ lb (1.6 kg) boneless pork butt roast, trimmed and cut into 1-inch (2.5-cm) cubes

1 ½ tbsp (10 g) ground cumin

1 tbsp (6 g) ground coriander

1 tbsp (3 g) dried Mexican oregano

1 tbsp (12 g) House Seasoning (page 193)

½ medium yellow onion, diced

1 (16-oz [453-g]) jar salsa verde

3 (4-oz [113-g]) cans diced mild green chiles

8 cloves garlic, minced

2 medium jalapeños, minced (seeds and membranes left intact for spicy, removed for mild), plus more for serving

½ cup (25 g) chopped fresh cilantro leaves, plus more for serving

Salt and freshly ground black pepper, to taste

Shredded pepper Jack cheese, for serving

Sliced avocado, for serving

12 (8-inch [20-cm]) warm flour tortillas, for serving

Sour cream, for serving

Place the pork cubes in a large slow cooker. Sprinkle with the cumin, coriander, Mexican oregano and House Seasoning. Top the pork cubes with the onion, salsa verde, diced green chiles, garlic and jalapeños. Stir to combine the ingredients, cover the slow cooker and cook on low for 8 to 10 hours, or on high for 4 to 5 hours, until the pork is tender. Stir in the cilantro and adjust the seasoning to taste with salt and pepper.

Serve the pork in a bowl topped with additional cilantro, pepper Jack cheese and sliced avocado with the warm flour tortillas on the side. To cool things down a bit, add a dollop of the sour cream.

# GERMAN ROULADEN-STYLE BEEF CUTLETS

Growing up with a German mother, I always looked forward to holiday dinners at our house for one main reason: rouladen! Rouladen is a traditional German recipe in which thin slices of beef are rolled around a filling of bacon, onions, pickles and mustard. We always enjoyed our rouladen over homemade spätzle: small, noodle-like dumplings native to the Swabian region of Germany where my mom's family still lives to this day. But while I've not yet been able to replicate spätzle in the slow cooker, my mom was floored by the fact that this recipe tastes *just like rouladen*. In fact, the flavor is so authentic and the preparation so much easier than the real deal that I may have heard my mother whisper the phrase, "I'm never going to make it the other way again." We shall see. In the meantime, this recipe involves no pounding of beef, no wrapping of filling and no browning of rolls. Rather, I took the original ingredients from the traditional dish and gave them a slightly different treatment. So here you have it—cutlets of beef in a scrumptious gravy that's resplendent with bacon, onions, pickles and, yes, even a touch of mustard. It's like Christmas dinner at Oma's house . . . and boy, is it tasty!

### YIELD: 6 SERVINGS

6 slices bacon, divided (about 6 oz [170 g] total)

2 tbsp (30 ml) vegetable oil, plus more as needed

2 lb (910 g) boneless beef round roast, sliced against the grain into ¾-inch (2-cm) thick cutlets

House Seasoning (page 193), to taste

1 medium yellow onion, cut into ¼-inch (6-mm) thick slices

6 oz (170 g) dill pickles, cut into ¼-inch (6-mm) thick slices

2 tbsp (30 g) stone-ground mustard

2 cups (480 ml) low-sodium beef broth

1 dried bay leaf

3 tbsp (24 g) cornstarch plus 3 tbsp (45 ml) water

Hot cooked spätzle or egg noodles, for serving

Minced fresh parsley, for serving

Cut 3 slices of the bacon into ½-inch (13-mm) pieces. In a large pot or Dutch oven, cook the bacon over medium-high heat until it is crispy. With a slotted spoon, transfer the bacon to a paper towel–lined plate to drain, leaving the remaining bacon grease in the pot. Add the vegetable oil to the pot and heat it until it is shimmering. Generously sprinkle both sides of the beef cutlets with the House Seasoning to taste. Working in batches, brown the beef cutlets 3 to 4 minutes per side, adding additional oil to the pot as necessary.

Chop, cover and refrigerate the cooked bacon, and transfer the browned beef to a large slow cooker. Top the beef with the onions, pickles and the 3 remaining slices of uncooked bacon. Dollop the stone-ground mustard into the slow cooker, pour the beef broth over the top and add the bay leaf. Cover the slow cooker and cook on low for 7 to 9 hours, or on high for 3 ½ to 4 ½ hours, until the beef is tender.

In a small bowl, mix the cornstarch and water until smooth and set aside. Transfer the beef cutlets to a plate, remove and discard the bacon slices from the slow cooker, and gently stir in the cornstarch slurry. Return the beef to the slow cooker, cover the slow cooker and cook on high for 15 minutes, until the gravy is thickened. Remove and discard the bay leaf. Serve the beef cutlets over the spätzle or egg noodles, garnish with the reheated chopped cooked bacon and top with plenty of the minced parsley.

# CHICKEN ALFREDO TORTELLINI

Chicken Alfredo is rather decadent as an everyday dinner, but for special occasions, it's an indulgent and easy-to-make treat. This recipe combines chunks of juicy chicken and tender cheese tortellini in a creamy, Parmesan-loaded, parsley-flecked Alfredo sauce. But the best part is that it pretty much makes itself! I always keep frozen tortellini on hand for convenience, but refrigerated tortellini will work just as well in this recipe if that's what you have available.

YIELD: 6 SERVINGS

1 ½ lb (680 g) boneless, skinless chicken breasts, trimmed

1 tbsp (12 g) House Seasoning (page 193)

4 cloves garlic, minced

2 ½ cups (600 ml) low-sodium chicken broth

1 ¼ cups (300 ml) heavy cream, at room temperature

½ cup (60 g) all-purpose flour

2 tbsp (28 g) butter

1 (19-oz [538-g]) bag frozen cheese tortellini, thawed

¾ cup (135 g) freshly grated Parmesan cheese, plus more for serving

½ cup (25 g) minced fresh parsley, plus more for serving

⅛ tsp ground nutmeg

Salt and freshly ground black pepper, to taste

Place the chicken breasts in the bottom of a large slow cooker. Sprinkle the chicken breasts with the House Seasoning. Add the garlic and pour the chicken broth into the bottom of the slow cooker. Cover the slow cooker and cook on low for 3 to 4 hours, until the chicken is tender and cooked through but not dry. Transfer the chicken breasts to a plate and cut or pull them into chunks and set aside. If desired, use a slotted spoon or sieve to skim off any "foam" from the broth in the slow cooker.

Add the heavy cream to a medium bowl and whisk in the flour until smooth. Pour the cream mixture into the slow cooker and stir. Add the chicken back to the slow cooker. Add the butter and tortellini, stirring to combine. Cover the slow cooker and cook on high for 30 minutes or until the sauce is thickened and the tortellini is tender, stirring halfway through. Stir in the Parmesan, parsley and nutmeg, and adjust the seasonings with additional salt and pepper to taste. Serve the Chicken Alfredo Tortellini garnished with additional Parmesan and parsley.

# SLOPPY JOE MEATLOAF

If you had to pick just one, would you choose sloppy joes or meatloaf? Well, why should you have to decide when you can have the best of both worlds? This yummy recipe is the result of glazing simple meatloaf with my tried and true sloppy joe sauce. The sauce is a little bit sweet, a little bit tangy and the perfect accompaniment to fork-tender slices of classic meatloaf. This recipe is sure to be a hit with kids and adults alike!

YIELD: 6 TO 8 SERVINGS

### SAUCE

1 (8-oz [228-g]) can tomato sauce

½ cup (118 ml) all-natural ketchup

1 tbsp (15 ml) honey

2 tbsp (30 ml) Worcestershire sauce

1 tsp (5 ml) prepared yellow mustard

1 tsp (4 g) House Seasoning (page 193)

Freshly ground black pepper, to taste

### MEATLOAF

2 lb (910 g) lean ground beef (90 percent lean)

2 cloves garlic, minced

1 cup (120 g) unseasoned dried or fresh breadcrumbs

½ cup (120 ml) milk

2 eggs

1 tbsp (12 g) House Seasoning (page 193)

Line the bottom of a large oval slow cooker with a foil sling (see Samantha's Tip). In a medium bowl, whisk together the tomato sauce, ketchup, honey, Worcestershire sauce, prepared yellow mustard, House Seasoning and black pepper. Pour half of the sauce into another small bowl. Cover and refrigerate one bowl of sauce and set the other aside.

In a large bowl, thoroughly combine the ground beef, garlic, breadcrumbs, milk, eggs and House Seasoning. Gently shape the meat mixture into an oval loaf and fit it into the bottom of the slow cooker. Spoon the sauce from unrefrigerated bowl over the meatloaf, keeping it mainly on top and just running down the sides (so that the excess doesn't burn on the bottom of the slow cooker). Cover the slow cooker and cook on low for 4 to 6 hours, or on high for 3 to 5 hours, until the meatloaf is fully cooked and a thermometer inserted into the center of the meatloaf measures 160°F (71°C).

Use the foil sling to carefully remove the meatloaf from the slow cooker. Transfer it to a cutting board or platter. Warm the reserved bowl of sauce and spoon another layer of it over the meatloaf. Tent the meatloaf with foil and allow it to rest for 15 minutes before slicing and serving with the remaining sauce on the side.

### Samantha's Tip

To make a foil sling, fold a long piece of heavy-duty foil to the width of the slow cooker and lay it along the bottom so that the edges extend up the sides and stick out the top. Repeat with another piece of foil laying the other direction, so that the foil pieces make a cross.

# LEMON-DILL POACHED SALMON

Salmon may not be the first protein that comes to mind when you think of slow cooker recipes, but the slow cooker can actually create an ideal, gentle environment for poaching fish. The only work involved in this recipe is whipping up the Creamy Dill Sauce and putting together the poaching stock in the morning or mid-day. Then simply allow the stock to slow cook for hours so that the aromatics can infuse the poaching liquid with flavor. When it's close to dinnertime, pop the salmon into the slow cooker, allow it to poach while you prepare the rest of the meal, and get ready for moist, tender, delicately flavored salmon!

YIELD: 4 SERVINGS

## POACHING STOCK

1 cup (240 ml) water

2 cups (480 ml) low-sodium vegetable broth

1 cup (240 ml) dry white wine (such as Chardonnay or Pinot Grigio)

1 lemon, cut into ¼-inch (6-mm) thick slices

2 shallots, cut into ⅛-inch (3-mm) thick slices

1 tbsp (9 g) capers

4 sprigs fresh dill

1 tsp (6 g) salt

15 black peppercorns

## CREAMY DILL SAUCE

⅓ cup (76 g) Greek yogurt

⅓ cup (70 g) sour cream

1 ½ tbsp (5 g) minced fresh dill

1 tsp (3 g) minced fresh parsley

1 tsp (5 ml) apple cider vinegar

1 tsp (4 g) House Seasoning (page 193)

Salt and freshly ground black pepper, to taste

4 skin-on salmon fillets (24 oz [680 g] total; 1- to 1 ½-inches [2.5- to 4-cm] thick)

Salt and freshly ground black pepper, to taste

Lemon wedges, for serving

In the bottom of a large oval slow cooker, combine the water, vegetable broth, white wine, lemon slices, shallots, capers, dill sprigs, salt and peppercorns. Cover the slow cooker and cook on low for 4 to 8 hours.

Prepare the Creamy Dill Sauce by whisking together the Greek yogurt, sour cream, dill, parsley, apple cider vinegar and House Seasoning in a small bowl. Adjust the seasoning with salt and pepper to taste, if desired. Cover the bowl and refrigerate the sauce for at least 1 hour, preferably longer, before serving.

Season the fleshy sides of the salmon fillets with salt and pepper to taste and place them in the slow cooker, skin-side down. Cover the slow cooker and cook on high for 20 to 40 minutes, until the salmon is flaky and opaque, with the thickest part of the fillets measuring 145°F (63°C) on an instant-read thermometer. If your salmon fillets are thin or your slow cooker runs hot, check for doneness sooner. Serve the salmon fillets with the lemon wedges and Creamy Dill Sauce.

# MEDITERRANEAN STUFFED BELL PEPPERS

Stuffed bell peppers are a fun, different and healthy way to enjoy ground beef. Just like stuffed peppers prepared in the oven, the meat in these peppers isn't precooked; rather, the peppers and their filling are simultaneously cooked in the slow cooker. I thought it would be fun to infuse these peppers with Mediterranean flavors, so instead of the typical rice and cheddar, these peppers feature couscous, diced tomatoes, Kalamata olives and feta cheese, with garnishes of Greek yogurt and chopped fresh basil for good measure. And while any color bell pepper will work, I prefer using red, orange or yellow bell peppers, which not only look festive but also tend to turn sweeter than the green ones as they cook.

YIELD: 6 SERVINGS

¾ cup (180 ml) water

¼ tsp salt

¾ cup (126 g) uncooked couscous

6 medium red, orange or yellow bell peppers

1 lb (455 g) lean ground beef (90 percent lean)

1 (14.5-oz [411-g]) can fire-roasted diced tomatoes

2 cloves garlic, minced

¾ cup (115 g) Kalamata olives, pitted and chopped

1 ¼ cups (6 oz [170 g]) crumbled feta cheese

1 tbsp (12 g) House Seasoning (page 193)

½ tsp dried oregano

½ tsp ground cumin

½ cup (100 g) Greek yogurt

Fresh basil chiffonade, for serving

Prepare the couscous by bringing the water and salt to a boil in a medium saucepan over high heat. Add the couscous and quickly stir. Remove the pot from the heat, cover it and allow the couscous to sit for 5 minutes before fluffing it with a fork.

While the couscous is cooking, wash the bell peppers and slice off their tops. Scoop out the seeds and membranes and set the peppers aside.

In a large bowl, combine the ground beef, cooked couscous, diced tomatoes, garlic, Kalamata olives, feta, House Seasoning, oregano and cumin. Divide the beef mixture evenly between the hollowed-out peppers, packing it down into the cavities. Arrange the upright stuffed peppers in a large oval slow cooker. Cover the slow cooker and cook on low for 4 to 6 hours, or on high for 2 to 3 hours, until the beef is cooked through (internal temperature of 160°F [71°C]). Carefully transfer the cooked peppers to a platter. Dollop or drizzle the Greek yogurt over the peppers (see Samantha's Tip). Sprinkle the peppers with the fresh basil and serve hot.

## Samantha's Tip

For a special presentation, you can drizzle Greek yogurt over the cooked stuffed peppers. Simply stir the yogurt until it is smooth, scoop it into a plastic zip-top bag, and snip a tiny piece off of one corner with scissors to create a piping bag for the yogurt. This trick can be used to garnish soups and chilis as well, and it also works with sour cream.

# SOUP'S ON!

## Fifteen Cozy Soup Recipes

Soup is a staple at our house—not only once the cool weather hits but year-round. There's just something so satisfying about warm, filling soup, which can be simple and straightforward or loaded with a variety of ingredients. Soup is ideal for comforting, and it's perfect for sharing. No matter the recipe, soup is as good for the soul as it is for the belly.

Lightened-Up Tomato Basil Soup (page 83) and grilled cheese sandwiches are a family favorite on a cozy Saturday afternoon. And when someone is battling the sniffles, Lemony Chicken Orzo Soup with Dill (page 100) comes to the rescue with nourishing broth and a boost of citrus.

In this chapter, I even share some easy-to-prepare soup recipes inspired by more complicated-to-make dinnertime entrées. In the mood for Italian? Serve up a bowl of Chicken Parmesan Soup (page 95) topped with plenty of cheese. Love the combination of ham, Swiss and chicken, but dislike the tedious work of rolling them all together with little toothpicks? Make mouthwatering Chicken Cordon Bleu Soup (page 84) instead. Craving soup that tastes like a comfort-food casserole classic? Zesty King Ranch Chicken Soup (page 87) is the answer. There's even Bacon Cheeseburger Soup (page 88) that—you guessed it!—tastes just like a cheeseburger, right down to the hamburger-bun croutons.

One of my favorite things about soup is how it's often an entire meal in one pot. But ultimately? Soup is love, and that's how I hope you end up feeling about these fifteen *soup-er* (sorry) slow cooker wonders.

# CHICKEN POT PIE SOUP
# WITH PIE CRUST DIPPERS

I first sampled chicken pot pie soup a couple of summers ago at a little al fresco restaurant high in the Colorado Rockies. Even though it was midsummer, when I picked up the menu and saw that one of my all-time favorite foods had been turned into soup, I couldn't *not* try it. I savored my comforting, veggie-loaded soup and, of course, the melt-in-your-mouth pie crust draped over the top! This effortless slow cooker version features my tried and true pie crust recipe turned into flaky, buttery Pie Crust Dippers, which end up being a perfect complement to the hearty, pot pie–mimicking soup.

### YIELD: 8 TO 10 SERVINGS

---

### SOUP

2 ½ lb (1.1 kg) bone-in, skin-on chicken breasts and thighs

1 lb (454 g) yellow potatoes, peeled and cut into ½-inch (13-mm) pieces

3 medium carrots, peeled and cut into ½-inch (13-mm) pieces

2 medium stalks celery, finely chopped

3 cloves garlic, minced

1 tbsp (12 g) House Seasoning (page 193)

2 tsp (3 g) Poultry Seasoning (page 194)

½ tsp dried thyme

2 dried bay leaves

7 cups (1.7 L) low-sodium chicken broth

⅔ cup (75 g) all-purpose flour

1 ½ cups (360 ml) half-and-half, at room temperature

2 to 3 tsp (10 to 15 ml) medium-dry or dry sherry, optional

2 cups (267 g) frozen peas, thawed

¼ cup (12 g) chopped fresh parsley

Salt and freshly ground black pepper, to taste

Place the chicken in a large slow cooker. Top the chicken with the potatoes, carrots, celery, garlic, House Seasoning, Poultry Seasoning, thyme and bay leaves. Add the chicken broth, stirring to combine. Cover the slow cooker and cook on low for 6 to 8 hours, until the chicken and vegetables are tender but not overcooked.

While the soup is cooking, prepare the Pie Crust Dippers. Pulse the butter, flour and salt in a food processor until the mixture resembles coarse sand with some small lumps of butter (no larger than pea-size) remaining. Pour the ice water, 1 tablespoon (15 ml) at a time, through the feed tube of the food processor, pulsing 4 to 5 times after each addition. Stop adding water when the mixture begins to form large clumps and pulls away from the sides of the food processor bowl.

Transfer the mixture onto a work surface and push it into a big lump using your hands. Quickly form the dough into a ball and flatten it into a 4-inch (10-cm) disk. Place the disk in a plastic zip-top bag or wrap it in plastic wrap and refrigerate it for at least 1 hour.

Preheat the oven to 425°F (220°C). Remove the dough from the refrigerator 3 to 4 minutes ahead of time, so that it just starts to soften and is easier to roll. Place the dough on a sheet of lightly floured parchment paper and flour the rolling pin as well. Roll out the disk of dough from the center, moving outward, turning it a quarter turn and repeating until the whole crust is about 12 inches (30 cm) in diameter. If the edges of the crust start to split, pinch them together before continuing. Sprinkle the crust with the Poultry Seasoning and freshly ground black pepper to taste. Using a knife, pizza cutter or fluted pastry wheel, cut the crust into 12 wedges. Slide the crust-topped parchment paper onto a baking sheet and bake for 11 to 13 minutes or until the Pie Crust Dippers are light golden brown. Set them aside to cool.

## PIE CRUST DIPPERS

½ cup (113 g) unsalted butter, cut into ¼-inch (6-mm) pieces and chilled

1 cup (125 g) plus 2 tbsp (16 g) all-purpose flour

½ tsp salt

4 to 5 tbsp (60 to 75 ml) ice water

Poultry Seasoning (page 194), to taste

Freshly ground black pepper, to taste

When the soup is done cooking, transfer the chicken to a cutting board and discard the bay leaves. Remove the skin, bones and any cartilage from the chicken and discard them. Chop the chicken into bite-size pieces and return it to the slow cooker.

In a medium bowl, whisk the flour into the half-and-half until smooth. Stir the half-and-half mixture into the slow cooker along with the sherry, peas and parsley. Cover the slow cooker and cook on high for 30 minutes or until the broth is thickened. Adjust the seasoning with salt and freshly ground black pepper to taste, if desired. Garnish with additional parsley and serve with the Pie Crust Dippers crumbled over the top.

See photo on page 78.

# LIGHTENED-UP TOMATO BASIL SOUP

I first fell in love with tomato basil soup at a certain French café chain restaurant, where it was thick, rich and ridiculously decadent. I learned to whip up a pretty good copycat at home, but over time, I started to feel rather guilty about the pint (475 ml) of cream and pound (450 g) of butter involved. So I decided to see if I could replicate my beloved recipe while lightening things up! This version replaces heavy cream with full-fat Greek yogurt for a rich flavor and silky texture with significantly reduced fat. Even my initially skeptical husband was sold on it after he tasted that first bite! Just be sure to temper the Greek yogurt before adding it to the hot soup, as it may curdle otherwise. Even if you forget that step, an additional spin with the immersion blender should smooth things out just fine. Finally, since canned tomatoes can vary in their sweetness and acidity, a bit of butter melted at the end of this recipe mellows out any lingering acidity. But if all else fails, adding ½ teaspoon sugar at a time (tasting at each interval, so as not to end up with overly sweet soup) should do the trick.

YIELD: 6 TO 8 SERVINGS

3 (14.5-oz [411-g]) cans crushed tomatoes

2 cups (480 ml) low-sodium chicken broth or vegetable broth

2 tbsp (30 ml) honey

½ cup (20 g) packed fresh basil leaves, roughly chopped, plus more for serving

½ tsp salt, plus more to taste

1 cup (227 g) full-fat Greek yogurt

2 tbsp (28 g) butter

Freshly ground black pepper, to taste

Combine the crushed tomatoes, chicken or vegetable broth, honey, basil and salt in a large slow cooker. Cover the slow cooker and cook on low for 4 to 6 hours.

Use an immersion blender to purée the soup until completely smooth. Measure the Greek yogurt into a medium bowl and temper it to prevent curdling by adding a small amount of hot soup to the bowl while continuously stirring the yogurt. Repeat this process several times to gradually bring up the temperature of the yogurt. Once the yogurt is warm, stir the mixture back into the soup. Add the butter. Season the soup with salt and freshly ground black pepper to taste. Cover the slow cooker and cook for 15 minutes, until heated through. Stir the soup well and serve garnished with chopped fresh basil.

# CHICKEN CORDON BLEU SOUP

It's probably evident by now that I rather enjoy turning my most beloved main course dishes into soups. And let me tell you, the authentic flavor of this soup is *spot-on*. Through most of my childhood, I actually would have picked chicken cordon bleu as my very favorite dinner. It's true that Swiss cheese and white wine may have been rather sophisticated tastes for an eight-year-old's palate, but hey, it was tasty then and it's just as amazing now! *Especially* in a version that doesn't involve pounding chicken and rolling up little bundles . . . or attempting to avoid the ingestion of toothpicks.

YIELD: 6 SERVINGS

8 tbsp (113 g) butter

2 cloves garlic, minced

½ cup (60 g) all-purpose flour

2 ½ cups (600 ml) low-sodium chicken broth

1 ½ cups (360 ml) dry white wine (such as Chardonnay or Pinot Grigio)

1 tbsp (12 g) House Seasoning (page 193)

½ tsp dried thyme

1 ½ lb (680 g) boneless, skinless chicken breasts

1 ½ cups (216 g) diced ham, cut into ½-inch (13-mm) cubes

2 cups (8 oz [160 g]) shredded Swiss cheese

1 cup (240 ml) half-and-half

¼ cup (12 g) minced fresh parsley, plus more for serving

Melt the butter in a medium saucepan over medium-low heat. Add the garlic and sauté until it is fragrant and light golden brown, about 1 minute. Stir in the flour and whisk continuously for 1 minute. Remove the saucepan from the heat and slowly and gradually whisk in the chicken broth and white wine. Return the pan to the stove, increase the heat to a simmer and whisk continuously for several minutes, until the sauce is smooth and thickened. Remove the saucepan from the heat, stir in the House Seasoning and thyme, and set the sauce aside.

Place the chicken breasts in a large slow cooker. Pour the sauce over the top. Cover the slow cooker and cook on low for 4 to 6 hours, until the chicken is tender and cooked through but not overcooked. Transfer the chicken to a cutting board. Add the ham cubes, Swiss cheese, half-and-half and parsley to the slow cooker, stirring to combine, and cover the slow cooker for the time being. Cut the chicken into bite-size cubes and slowly stir it back into the slow cooker. Cover the slow cooker and cook for 15 minutes, until the Swiss cheese is melted and all of the ingredients are heated through. Stir well and serve with extra parsley, if desired.

# KING RANCH CHICKEN SOUP

King Ranch Chicken Casserole—with no ties to its famous south-Texas namesake—is zippy, creamy, cheesy comfort food at its finest. It's also a delicacy that I wasn't actually privy to until college, since my German-born mother was too busy feeding us things like lentils and spätzle to have time for Southern delicacies. Nevertheless, I'll be forever grateful to my college roomie for introducing me to the best casserole ever. And believe me when I say that I've made up for lost time eating it since then. In fact, I adore it so much that I turned it into a soup that tastes just like the casserole. And I know y'all will love it, too!

## YIELD: 6 SERVINGS

---

8 tbsp (113 g) butter

2 cloves garlic, minced

½ cup (60 g) all-purpose flour

4 cups (1 L) low-sodium chicken broth

4 tsp (11 g) chili powder

1 tbsp (7 g) ground cumin

1 tbsp (10 g) garlic powder

1 tsp (6 g) salt

Freshly ground black pepper, to taste

1 ½ lb (680 g) boneless, skinless chicken breasts

1 (10-oz [283-g]) can diced tomatoes with green chiles (mild, original or hot, depending on your heat preference)

1 medium jalapeño, minced (seeds and membranes left intact for spicy, removed for mild)

2 cups (8 oz [230 g]) shredded sharp cheddar, Mexican blend or Colby Jack cheese, plus more for serving

Tortilla chips, for serving

Chopped fresh cilantro, for serving, optional

Melt the butter in a medium saucepan over medium-low heat. Add the garlic and sauté until it is fragrant and light golden brown, about 1 minute. Stir in the flour and whisk continuously for 1 minute. Slowly whisk in the chicken broth. Increase the heat to a simmer and whisk continuously for several minutes, until the sauce is smooth and thickened. Remove the saucepan from the heat, and stir in the chili powder, cumin, garlic powder and salt. Add black pepper to taste and set the sauce aside.

Place the chicken breasts in a large slow cooker. Top them with the diced tomatoes with green chiles and jalapeño and pour the sauce over the top. Cover the slow cooker and cook on low for 4 to 6 hours, until the chicken is tender and cooked through but not overcooked. Transfer the chicken to a cutting board, stir the cheese into the slow cooker and cover the slow cooker for the time being. Pull the chicken into large chunks and stir it back into the slow cooker. Cover the slow cooker and cook for 15 minutes, until the cheese is melted and all of the ingredients are heated through. Stir well. To serve, crush the tortilla chips into a bowl and ladle the soup over the top, garnishing with extra cheese and the cilantro, if desired.

# BACON CHEESEBURGER SOUP

When I was developing cookbook recipes, this one ranked right up there in my kids' top five. It makes total sense in the case of my eldest—I constantly craved cheeseburgers when I was pregnant with him and they've been his favorite thing to eat ever since he was big enough to scarf one down. But this soup went over well with the entire family. They even changed the lyrics of a certain song to *cheeseburger in paradise . . . soup!* I've seen other cheeseburger soup recipes that include ingredients like chopped carrots and celery. But I don't eat those things on my cheeseburgers, so I decided that they didn't have any place in this soup! Instead, I went with a creamy potato base (think French fries, people), added the obligatory cooked ground beef and cheddar, and achieved that classic cheeseburger flavor with some don't-leave-'em-off garnishes: tomatoes, onions and, yes, even pickles! Oh, and of course there's the bacon—don't ever underestimate the power of bacon.

YIELD: 6 TO 8 SERVINGS

---

2 lb (910 g) russet potatoes, peeled and cut into 2-inch (5-cm) pieces

4 cloves garlic, minced

5 cups (1.2 L) low-sodium chicken broth

1 tbsp (12 g) House Seasoning (page 193), plus more to season croutons and beef

3 hamburger buns, with or without sesame seeds

4 tbsp (60 ml) butter, melted

1 lb (454 g) lean ground beef (90 percent lean)

8 slices bacon (about 8 oz [227 g])

4 cups (16 oz [454 g]) shredded extra-sharp cheddar cheese, plus more for serving

1 cup (240 ml) half-and-half

Salt and freshly ground black pepper, to taste

Chopped tomatoes, for serving

Thinly sliced onions, for serving

Diced pickles, for serving

Combine the potatoes, garlic, chicken broth and House Seasoning in a large slow cooker. Cover the slow cooker and cook on low for 6 to 8 hours, or on high for 3 to 4 hours, until the potatoes are completely tender.

While the potatoes are cooking, prepare the croutons. Preheat the oven to 350°F (177°C). Cut the hamburger buns into 1-inch (2.5-cm) cubes. Toss the cubes in a gallon-size plastic zip-top bag with the butter, spread them into a single layer on a large baking sheet and sprinkle them with the House Seasoning to taste. Bake the croutons for 5 minutes, shake the baking sheet to flip the croutons, and bake them 5 to 10 more minutes until they are light golden brown. Set the croutons aside to cool.

Shortly before the potatoes are done, brown the ground beef in a large saucepan set over medium-high heat until it is cooked through. Drain the grease and season the beef with the House Seasoning to taste.

To cook the bacon, position the oven rack in the center of the oven and preheat the oven to 400°F (204°C). Cover a large, rimmed baking sheet with heavy-duty aluminum foil and line it with the bacon. Cook the bacon for 15 to 20 minutes, or until it is crispy. Use a fork or tongs to remove the bacon to a paper towel–lined plate to drain. Chop the drained bacon and set it aside.

Once the potatoes are cooked, use an immersion blender to purée the soup until smooth. Gradually stir the cheddar into the slow cooker until it is completely melted, and then mix in the half-and-half. Stir in the cooked ground beef and half of the cooked bacon. Season with salt and pepper to taste and, if desired, thin out the soup with a splash of additional broth or half-and-half, but only if it seems too thick. Cover the slow cooker and cook on low for 5 to 10 minutes, until the soup is just heated through, but not too long or the soup may start to darken around the edges. Serve the soup topped with the croutons, additional cheddar, remaining chopped bacon, chopped tomatoes, sliced onions and diced pickles.

# TUSCAN WHITE BEAN SOUP

Cozy, creamy and bursting with flavor, this white bean soup is like a taste of Tuscany! While I love puréeing the entire pot to a smooth, silky consistency, it's also possible to leave some texture intact if that's your preference. In other words, you can either eat the soup in its whole-bean glory as soon as it finishes cooking, or you can scoop out half of the beans with a slotted spoon, purée what remains in the slow cooker and then add the whole beans back. If you do blend up all of the soup, however, it's okay to splash in some extra chicken broth to thin things out a bit. Finally, be sure to season your soup with salt and pepper before serving (salt at the beginning of the cooking time can toughen the beans, so it's best to save it for the end), and don't leave off the ever-important garnish—because if everything's better with bacon, this soup is *perfect* with pancetta!

YIELD: 4 TO 6 SERVINGS

---

1 lb (454 g) dried great Northern beans, picked over, rinsed and drained

4 cloves garlic, minced

7 cups (1.7 L) low-sodium chicken broth, plus more if desired

¾ tsp dried sage

¾ tsp dried rosemary

1 dried bay leaf

⅓ cup (54 g) freshly grated Parmesan cheese, plus more for serving

¼ cup (60 ml) half-and-half

1 ½ tsp (8 ml) white wine vinegar

Salt and freshly ground black pepper, to taste

2 oz (56 g) diced pancetta, cooked until crispy

Crusty Italian bread, for serving

Combine the beans, garlic, chicken broth, sage, rosemary and bay leaf in a large slow cooker. Cover the slow cooker and cook on low for 6 to 8 hours, until beans are very tender.

Discard the bay leaf and use an immersion blender to purée the soup until smooth. Blend in the Parmesan, half-and-half and white wine vinegar, and season with the salt, ¼ teaspoon at a time, and pepper to taste. If desired, adjust the consistency of the soup by blending in additional chicken broth or half-and-half. Cover the slow cooker and cook for 15 more minutes, until the soup is heated through.

To cook the pancetta, heat 1 tablespoon (15 ml) extra-virgin olive oil in a medium saucepan over medium heat. Add the diced pancetta and cook, stirring, for about 2 minutes or until it is crisp. Drain on a paper towel–lined plate. (If you prefer, cooked and chopped bacon may be substituted for the pancetta in this recipe.)

Serve the soup with additional Parmesan cheese, the diced pancetta on top and some crusty Italian bread on the side.

### Samantha's Tip

If you can't find dried great Northern beans for this recipe, you may substitute dried navy beans. However, do not use dried cannellini beans, a.k.a. white kidney beans, unless you are willing to pre-boil them on the stove first in order to ensure that they are safe to eat (see Red Beans and Rice on page 42 for Samantha's Tip regarding safe bean preparation).

# THAI SHRIMP SOUP WITH RICE NOODLES

This flavorful soup incorporates many flavors of the popular Thai soup, tom kha gai—but with a twist. I particularly love that this recipe is so customizable. Increase the mushrooms if you like. Whether you're sensitive to spice or can handle the heat, feel free to tweak the amount of red curry paste. If you'd prefer a richer soup, substitute extra coconut milk for some of the chicken broth. If you want to try this recipe with more traditional chicken instead of shrimp, simply swap 'em out. And I'll warn you now: slurping up the rice noodles in this soup can be a bit messy. So if you're not feeling up to using a big spoon and chopsticks, you even have my permission to trade the noodles for rice!

### YIELD: 6 TO 8 SERVINGS

8 oz (227 g) shiitake, oyster or white mushrooms, cleaned and cut into ¼-inch (13-mm) thick slices

6 cloves garlic, minced

3 tbsp (29 g) minced galangal (Thai ginger) or regular ginger

2 medium stalks lemongrass, optional

6 cups (1.4 L) low-sodium chicken broth

¼ cup (60 ml) fish sauce, plus more for serving

3 tbsp (45 ml) freshly squeezed lime juice

2 tbsp (30 g) Thai red curry paste, plus more for serving

1 tbsp (15 ml) honey

1 (13.5-oz [400-ml]) can full-fat coconut milk

8 oz (227 g) rice noodles (preferably the same width as pad thai noodles or fettuccine)

½ cup (25 g) chopped fresh cilantro, plus more for serving

1 lb (454 g) medium raw shrimp, peeled and deveined

Lime wedges, for serving

Combine the mushrooms, garlic, galangal or ginger, lemongrass (if using), chicken broth, fish sauce, lime juice, Thai red curry paste and honey in a large slow cooker. Cover the slow cooker and cook on low for 4 to 6 hours.

Discard the lemongrass stalks. Increase the heat to high and stir in the coconut milk, rice noodles and cilantro. Cover the slow cooker and cook for 15 to 30 minutes, until the noodles are tender, then turn off the slow cooker.

While the noodles are cooking, bring a large saucepan of lightly salted water to a boil over high heat. Add the shrimp, reduce the heat to a simmer and cook uncovered for 1 to 3 minutes, until the shrimp turn pink and opaque. Drain the shrimp and stir them into the slow cooker.

Serve the soup immediately, garnished with more cilantro, lime wedges, Thai red curry paste and fish sauce to taste.

VARIATIONS: Omit the shrimp. Instead, add two raw bone-in chicken breasts (skin-on or skinless) along with the mushrooms, garlic, galangal or ginger, lemongrass (if using), chicken broth, fish sauce, lime juice, Thai red curry paste and honey. After cooking for 4 to 6 hours, transfer the chicken to a cutting board, discard the bones and any skin, and chop or tear the chicken into bite-size pieces. Stir the chicken back into the soup after the noodles are done cooking.

Omit the rice noodles. Instead, cook 1 cup (180 g) jasmine rice according to package directions. Put some cooked rice in each individual bowl before ladling the soup on top.

# CHICKEN PARMESAN SOUP

If you like chicken Parmesan, you're going to *love* Chicken Parmesan Soup! Its seasoned tomatoey broth relies on the shortcut ingredient of jarred marinara sauce (just be sure to check the label for artificial ingredients), and there's no shortage of tender chicken, pasta and Parmesan to round things out. You can use any shape of pasta that suits your fancy, but measure it by *weight* instead of cups for accuracy (8 ounces [227 g] of differently shaped pastas may not measure out to the same number of cups; see page 14 for a full explanation). Also, if you're switching up the pasta, adjust the cooking time accordingly, depending on whether it's more delicate or heavy-duty than farfalle.

YIELD: 6 TO 8 SERVINGS

---

1 ½ lb (680 g) boneless, skinless chicken breasts

3 cloves garlic, minced

1 (24-oz [680-g]) jar marinara sauce

6 cups (1.4 L) low-sodium chicken broth

3 tbsp (50 g) tomato paste

1 tbsp (12 g) House Seasoning (page 193)

1 tbsp (3 g) Italian Seasoning (page 193)

¼ tsp fennel seeds, crushed

8 oz (227 g) dry farfalle (bowtie) pasta

1 cup (180 g) freshly grated Parmesan cheese, plus more for serving

Salt and freshly ground black pepper, to taste

Chopped fresh parsley or basil, for garnishing

Place the chicken breasts in a large slow cooker. Top them with the garlic, marinara sauce, chicken broth, tomato paste, House Seasoning, Italian Seasoning and fennel seeds, stirring to combine. Cover the slow cooker and cook on low for 4 to 6 hours or until the chicken is tender and cooked through but not overcooked.

When the soup is done cooking, transfer the chicken breasts to a cutting board and pull or chop them into large chunks. Stir the chicken and farfalle into the slow cooker and increase the heat to high. Cover the slow cooker and cook for 15 minutes, then stir the pasta and check it for doneness. If necessary, cover the slow cooker again and cook for a few minutes longer until the pasta is al dente.

Stir in the Parmesan and adjust the seasoning, adding salt and pepper if desired. Serve Chicken Parmesan Soup topped with additional Parmesan and a garnish of fresh parsley or basil.

## Samantha's Tip

It's a good idea to crush fennel seeds before adding them to a recipe to bring out their maximum flavor and aroma. If you have a mortar and pestle, great! If not, place them in a plastic zip-top bag, squeeze out the air and use the flat side of a meat mallet to gently crush them.

# SPLIT PEA SOUP WITH SAUSAGE

Hearty, healthy and filling, the split peas in this soup break down into a thick and creamy base for tender carrots and flavorful slices of sausage, or diced ham, if that's your preference. It's the perfect one-pot meal when it's cold outside and you could use a little comfort . . . and a happy tummy.

YIELD: 4 TO 6 SERVINGS

1 lb (454 g) dried green split peas, picked over, rinsed and drained

12 oz (340 g) smoked sausage (such as kielbasa), cut into ¼-inch (6-mm) slices

3 medium carrots, peeled and finely chopped

2 medium stalks celery, finely chopped

½ medium yellow onion, finely chopped

4 cloves garlic, minced

6 cups (1.4 L) low-sodium chicken broth, plus more if desired

2 tsp (8 g) House Seasoning (page 193)

1 tsp (15 ml) Worcestershire sauce

1 tsp (2 g) smoked paprika

¼ tsp hot sauce (such as Tabasco brand)

2 dried bay leaves

¼ cup (12 g) minced fresh parsley, plus more for serving

Salt and freshly ground black pepper, to taste

Apple cider vinegar, for serving

Combine the split peas, sausage, carrots, celery, onion, garlic, chicken broth, House Seasoning, Worcestershire sauce, smoked paprika, hot sauce and bay leaves in a large slow cooker. Cover the slow cooker and cook on low for 8 to 10 hours, or on high for 4 to 5 hours, until the split peas are tender and broken down. Discard the bay leaves and stir in the parsley. Season with salt and pepper to taste and, if desired, thin out the soup with a splash of additional broth, but only if it seems too thick. For extra pizzazz, stir ½ teaspoon apple cider vinegar into each bowl of soup before serving.

# BROCCOLI-POTATO CHEDDAR SOUP

What happens when you cross broccoli cheese soup with creamy potato soup? Why, you get a thick, cheesy hybrid with luxurious texture and extra vitamins! I typically purée this soup until completely smooth (the better to hide your broccoli with, my dear), but if you'd enjoy chunks of broccoli and potatoes, you can always pull some out with a slotted spoon before firing up the immersion blender and then add them back in later. Additionally, the amounts of potatoes and broccoli in this recipe can be tweaked (use more potatoes and less broccoli or vice versa), so long as the total amount of veggies stays about the same.

YIELD: 6 TO 8 SERVINGS

---

1 ½ lb (683 g) russet potatoes, peeled and cut into 2-inch (5-cm) pieces

20 oz (566 g) frozen broccoli florets, thawed

4 cloves garlic, minced

4 cups (1 L) low-sodium chicken broth or vegetable broth

2 tsp (8 g) House Seasoning (page 193)

3 cups (12 oz [340 g]) shredded sharp cheddar cheese, plus more for serving

¼ cup (45 g) freshly grated Parmesan cheese, plus more for serving

4 oz (112 g) cream cheese, cubed and at room temperature

1 cup (240 ml) whole milk

Salt and freshly ground black pepper, to taste

Combine the potatoes, broccoli florets, garlic, chicken broth and House Seasoning in a large slow cooker. Cover the slow cooker and cook on low for 6 to 8 hours or on high for 3 to 4 hours, until the potatoes are very tender.

Use an immersion blender to purée the soup until smooth. Gradually stir in the cheddar, Parmesan and cream cheese until melted, and then blend in the milk. Season with salt and pepper to taste and, if desired, thin out the soup with a splash of additional broth or milk (only if it seems too thick). Cover the slow cooker and cook on low for 10 minutes, until heated through, and stir the soup well before serving it topped with extra cheddar and Parmesan.

# LEMONY CHICKEN ORZO SOUP WITH DILL

Regular ol' chicken noodle soup gets a vibrant makeover with the flavors of fresh lemon and dill. And let's not forget those cute little pieces of orzo pasta bobbing around! Orzo can be a bit too persnickety for the slow cooker, so your best bet is to cook it on the stove just before the soup is done and then stir it into the awaiting lemony chicken deliciousness. If you crave an even more prominent lemon flavor in this soup, feel free to add extra lemon juice 1 tablespoon (15 ml) at a time, to be safe, or you can even toss in a bit of lemon zest.

YIELD: 8 TO 10 SERVINGS

2 ½ lb (1.1 kg) bone-in, skin-on chicken breasts and thighs

3 medium carrots, peeled and finely chopped

½ medium yellow onion, finely chopped

3 cloves garlic, minced

1 tbsp (12 g) House Seasoning (page 193)

1 tsp (2 g) dried parsley

¼ tsp dried thyme

1 dried bay leaf

8 cups (2 L) low-sodium chicken broth

8 oz (227 g) orzo pasta, cooked in salted water according to package directions until al dente and drained

¼ cup (60 ml) freshly squeezed lemon juice

¼ cup (12 g) chopped fresh dill, plus more for serving

Salt and freshly ground black pepper, to taste

Place the chicken a large slow cooker. Top the chicken with the carrots, onion, garlic, House Seasoning, parsley, thyme and bay leaf. Pour the chicken broth into the slow cooker and stir to combine. Cover the slow cooker and cook on low for 6 to 8 hours, until the chicken and vegetables are tender but not overcooked.

When the soup is done cooking, discard the bay leaf and transfer the chicken to a cutting board. Remove the skin, bones and any cartilage from the chicken and discard them. Pull the chicken into large chunks and return them to the slow cooker. Stir in the cooked orzo, lemon juice and fresh dill, and season to taste with salt and pepper. Cover the slow cooker and cook for 5 to 10 minutes, until the soup is heated through. Serve garnished with more dill.

# CREAMY ITALIAN TORTELLINI SOUP

This comforting, flavorful soup boasts a variety of flavors, textures and colors, all co-existing in perfect harmony in a creamy broth. Many people think of Italian sausage as sold in links with casings, but you can actually find it in bulk packages in the meat case, or behind the butcher counter, as well, making it easy to brown up in a recipe like this. I typically thaw my frozen tortellini in a colander under warm running water, but you may substitute refrigerated tortellini in this recipe if you prefer—just watch the cooking time in case it needs to be slightly reduced.

YIELD: 6 TO 8 SERVINGS

1 lb (454 g) bulk Italian sausage (sweet, spicy or a combination)

4 cloves garlic, minced

1 (14.5-oz [411-g]) can fire-roasted diced tomatoes, undrained

1 (14-oz [396-g]) can quartered artichoke hearts, drained

1 tbsp (12 g) House Seasoning (page 193)

1 tbsp (3 g) Italian Seasoning (page 193)

4 cups (1 L) low-sodium chicken broth

1 (16-oz [454-g]) bag frozen cheese tortellini, thawed

1 ½ cups (360 ml) half-and-half

½ cup (90 g) freshly grated Parmesan cheese, plus more for serving

4 oz (115 g) fresh baby spinach, coarsely chopped

Salt and freshly ground black pepper, to taste

In a large saucepan over medium-high heat, brown the Italian sausage until it is cooked through, stirring in the garlic for the last 1 to 2 minutes. Drain the grease. Combine the cooked sausage and garlic, diced tomatoes, artichoke hearts, House Seasoning, Italian Seasoning and chicken broth in a large slow cooker. Cover the slow cooker and cook on low for 4 to 6 hours, or on high for 2 ½ to 3 hours.

Stir in the tortellini, half-and-half and Parmesan. Cover the slow cooker and cook on low for 1 hour, or on high for 30 minutes, until the tortellini is tender. Add the spinach, cover the slow cooker for about 5 more minutes until the spinach wilts, and gently stir to combine. Adjust the seasoning with salt and pepper, if desired, and serve the soup garnished with additional Parmesan.

# ZESTY CHICKEN, BLACK BEAN AND CORN SOUP

This effortless soup is loaded with chunks of tender chicken, creamy black beans and sweet corn in a taco-seasoned broth. It's easy to tweak it to your spice preferences by choosing mild, medium or hot salsa and, if you like, tossing in an extra can of green chiles or even some minced fresh jalapeños. But whatever you do, don't forget to load up your bowl with the (not-so-optional) garnishes! While tasty without them, this soup is even better swirled with sour cream and topped with plenty of crushed tortilla chips and extra cheese.

YIELD: 6 TO 8 SERVINGS

2 lb (910 g) bone-in, skin-on chicken breasts and thighs

12 oz (340 g) dried black beans, picked over, rinsed and drained

1 lb (454 g) frozen corn, thawed

6 cloves garlic, minced

1 (4-oz [113-g]) can diced mild green chiles

1 (16-oz [454-g]) jar salsa

3 tbsp (30 g) Taco Seasoning (page 194)

8 cups (2 L) low-sodium chicken broth

Sour cream, for serving

Tortilla chips, for serving

Shredded cheddar, Monterey Jack or Mexican blend cheese, for serving

Place the chicken in a large slow cooker. Top the chicken with the black beans, corn, garlic, green chiles and salsa. Sprinkle the chicken mixture with the Taco Seasoning, pour the chicken broth over the top, and stir to combine. Cover the slow cooker and cook on low for 8 to 10 hours, or on high for 4 to 5 hours, until the beans are completely tender.

When the soup is done cooking, transfer the chicken to a cutting board. Remove the skin, bones and any cartilage from the chicken and discard them. Pull the chicken into bite-size chunks and return it to the slow cooker. Stir the soup to combine, cover the slow cooker and cook for 5 to 10 more minutes, until the soup is heated through.

To serve, ladle the soup into a bowl, stir in a dollop of the sour cream, and top with a generous amount of crushed tortilla chips and shredded cheese.

# CARROT-THYME BISQUE

One of my favorite things to serve my kiddos for lunch on a chilly weekend is soup with grilled cheese sandwiches. That soup typically takes the form of tomato, but sometimes we get all wild and crazy with this carrot-loaded delight instead. Surprisingly, the secret to this recipe's success is the addition of just enough salt at the end. Without adequate salt, this soup is rather bland and boring. But once you reach the perfect amount of salt, the flavors suddenly *pop*! I recommend adding ¼ teaspoon at a time and tasting between intervals until it's just perfect. And while you're at it, don't forget the pepper!

YIELD: 6 TO 8 SERVINGS

2 ½ lb ([1.1 kg] about 15 medium carrots), peeled and cut into 1-inch (2.5-cm) pieces

6 cups (1.4 L) low-sodium vegetable broth or chicken broth

1 ½ tbsp (22 ml) maple syrup

1 tbsp (2.5 g) chopped fresh thyme or 1 tsp (1 g) dried thyme

½ tsp salt, plus more to taste

Freshly ground black pepper, to taste

1 cup (240 ml) half-and-half

1 ½ tsp (7 ml) white wine vinegar

Combine the carrots, vegetable or chicken broth, maple syrup, thyme, salt and pepper in a large slow cooker. Cover the slow cooker and cook on low for 8 to 10 hours, or on high for 4 to 5 hours, until the carrots are completely tender.

Use an immersion blender to purée the soup until smooth. Stir in the half-and-half and white wine vinegar, and season with additional salt and pepper to taste. Cover the slow cooker and cook on low for 10 to 15 minutes, until the soup is heated through.

# POTATO, SAUSAGE AND SPINACH SOUP

Requiring just a few minutes to toss into the slow cooker, this hearty combo of potatoes and smoked sausage is brightened by fresh baby spinach. For a heartier bite, you can substitute kale for the spinach if you like—just make sure to remove the tough stems and finely chop it first. (Incidentally, my kids are actually more likely to eat kale in their soup if I shred it in the food processor first and refer to it as parsley, but that's another story for another day.) Spinach or kale, the don't-wanna-miss-ingredient in this soup is, surprisingly, the feta cheese stirred in at the end, which somewhat melts into the soup to lend it a lovely creaminess—so don't skip it!

YIELD: 6 SERVINGS

2 lb (910 g) small red potatoes, peeled and cut into bite-size pieces

12 oz (340 g) smoked sausage (such as kielbasa), cut into ¼-inch (6-mm) slices

6 cloves garlic, minced

6 cups (1.4 L) low-sodium chicken broth

1 ½ tsp (6 g) House Seasoning (page 193)

1 dried bay leaf

⅛ tsp hot sauce (such as Tabasco brand)

5 oz (142 g) fresh baby spinach

Salt and freshly ground black pepper, to taste

1 ¼ cups (6 oz [170 g]) crumbled feta cheese

Combine the potatoes, sausage, garlic, chicken broth, House Seasoning, bay leaf and hot sauce in a large slow cooker. Cover the slow cooker and cook on low for 6 to 8 hours or until the potatoes are tender. Discard the bay leaf, add the spinach, cover the slow cooker for about 5 more minutes until the spinach wilts, and gently stir the soup to combine. Season with salt and pepper, if desired, and garnish each serving with a generous amount of crumbled feta cheese.

# STEWS, CHILIS AND CHOWDERS

## Twelve Thick and Hearty One-Bowl Dinners

Have you ever been in a soup sorta mood but you're also hankering for something a little bit thicker? Heartier? Chunkier? *That*, my friends, is where these recipes save the day!

Chunky doesn't always have to mean meat, mind you. This chapter includes three veggie-loaded options, including a zesty Tex-Mex Creamy Corn Chowder (page 119) that will knock your socks off.

If you're a fan of chili, there's no shortage of mouthwatering options in the upcoming pages. My family is actually split on which one to call our favorite. I find myself regularly craving tender, spicy Pulled-Pork Chili (page 120), my husband loves my Daddy's Texas Chili (page 127) for its straightforward ingredients and classic flavor, and my kids can't get enough yummy Beefy Three-Bean Chili (page 112). Needless to say, they're all in regular rotation at our house.

The next time stew sounds good, don't miss healthy, filling, toss-it-in-and-forget-it Beef and Barley Stew (page 132)—it's guaranteed to leave you smiling and satisfied. Or—if you're willing to put in a bit more work for complex layers of flavor—bacon and red wine–kissed Beef Bourguignon (page 124) is unbelievably delicious. And if you happen to enjoy lamb, there's even a stew for you! Irish Lamb and Potato Stew (page 112) is tasty on Saint Patrick's Day or any day of the year.

Finally, even though it's missing stew, chili or chowder in its name, the arguable star of this chapter is Chicken and Dumplings (page 116)! Because who wouldn't go crazy for succulent, fall-apart chicken and fluffy dumplings in a thick and flavorful broth?

Now, excuse me while I go fire up the slow cooker to get started on something from this chapter. Have fun deciding which one of these satisfying meals to try first!

# BEEFY THREE-BEAN CHILI

One of the fun things about chili is how many variations there are, and a steamy bowl of this beef and bean goodness doesn't disappoint! As usual, feel free to make it your own. Swap out any of the cans of beans for your favorite variety. If you wish, ground turkey, venison or bison (or even an extra can of beans) can change things up from beef. It's also easy to tweak the spice level to your liking with more or less of the canned chipotles in adobo—a little bit of chipotle goes a long way!

YIELD: 6 TO 8 SERVINGS

1 lb (454 g) lean ground beef (90 percent lean)

House Seasoning (page 193), to taste

2 (15-oz [425-g]) cans black beans, drained and rinsed

1 (15-oz [425-g]) can pinto beans, drained and rinsed

1 (15-oz [425-g]) can kidney beans, drained and rinsed

1 chipotle pepper in adobo sauce, minced

1 tsp (5 g) adobo sauce (more or less, to taste)

4 cloves garlic, minced

1 (14.5-oz [411-g]) can fire-roasted diced tomatoes

1 (12-oz [355-ml]) bottle dark beer (see page 17 for recommendations)

2 tbsp (16 g) chili powder

1 tbsp (7 g) ground cumin

1 tbsp (7 g) ground coriander

2 tsp (2 g) dried Mexican oregano

¼ tsp smoked paprika

Salt and freshly ground black pepper, to taste

Sour cream, for serving

Shredded cheddar, Monterey Jack or Mexican blend cheese, for serving

Chopped fresh cilantro, for serving

Brown the ground beef in a large saucepan over medium-high heat until it is cooked through. Drain the grease and season with the House Seasoning to taste.

In a large slow cooker, combine the cooked ground beef, black beans, pinto beans, kidney beans, chipotle pepper, adobo sauce, garlic, diced tomatoes, beer, chili powder, cumin, coriander, Mexican oregano and paprika. Cover the slow cooker and cook on low for 6 to 8 hours, or on high for 3 to 4 hours. Adjust the seasoning with additional salt and pepper, if desired. Serve with a dollop of sour cream, a pinch of shredded cheese and a sprinkle of cilantro.

# PORK AND HOMINY STEW

Reminiscent of the wonderful pork and hominy combo found in pozole, this somewhat spicy and highly flavorful medley is like a cross between a stew and a chili. And while the fresh poblanos may be impressive in size compared to other varieties of chile peppers, they're actually fairly mild. Rather, the heat in this dish primarily comes from the chipotle chile powder. Whether you like it spicy or mild, however, don't leave off the garnishes!

YIELD: 4 TO 6 SERVINGS

2 ½ lb (1.1 kg) boneless pork butt roast, trimmed and cut into 1 ½-inch (4-cm) cubes

1 tbsp (12 g) House Seasoning (page 193)

2 tsp (5 g) chili powder

1 tsp (2 g) chipotle chile powder

1 tsp (2 g) ground cumin

1 tsp (1 g) dried Mexican oregano

1 medium yellow onion, finely chopped

1 medium carrot, peeled and grated

6 cloves garlic, minced

2 medium poblano peppers, seeded and coarsely chopped

2 (15-oz [425-g]) cans golden hominy, drained and rinsed

1 (14.5-oz [411-g]) can fire-roasted diced tomatoes

1 (12-oz [355-ml]) bottle dark beer (see page 17 for recommendations)

¼ cup (30 g) all-purpose flour

1 cup (240 ml) low-sodium chicken broth

Diced avocado, for serving

Crumbled Cotija cheese, for serving

Chopped fresh cilantro, for serving

Freshly squeezed lime juice, for serving

Place the pork cubes in a large slow cooker. Sprinkle them with the House Seasoning, chili powder, chipotle chile powder, cumin and Mexican oregano, tossing the cubes to coat them. Add the onion, carrot, garlic, poblano peppers, hominy and diced tomatoes to the slow cooker. Slowly pour in the beer.

In a medium bowl, whisk the flour into the chicken broth until smooth, then pour the mixture into the slow cooker. Stir to combine all of the ingredients, cover the slow cooker and cook on low for 8 to 10 hours, or on high for 4 to 5 hours, until the pork is tender. Use a large spoon to skim the fat from the surface of the stew. Serve the stew topped with the avocado, Cotija, cilantro and a squeeze of lime.

# CHICKEN AND DUMPLINGS

Who's ready for a comfort-food classic? Because I think you'll agree that Chicken and Dumplings is the *quintessential* Southern comfort food. Many people are familiar with the slow cooker condensed soup/refrigerated biscuit version, but after you try this real-food delight, there will be no looking back. And this is the only recipe in the cookbook where I ask you to brown chicken ahead of time, but for good reason—it's worth it! Your efforts here will be richly rewarded with amazing flavor, luxurious broth and fluffy dumplings . . . *yum.*

YIELD: 6 SERVINGS

---

CHICKEN

1 tbsp (14 g) butter, plus more as needed

1 tbsp (15 ml) vegetable oil, plus more as needed

2 ½ lb (1.1 kg) bone-in, skin-on chicken breasts and thighs

House Seasoning (page 193), to taste

3 medium carrots, peeled and cut into ½-inch (13-mm) thick slices

2 medium stalks celery, finely chopped

3 garlic cloves, minced

1 ½ tsp (1 g) dried thyme

3 dried bay leaves

6 cups (1.4 L) low-sodium chicken broth

¼ cup (30 g) flour plus 1 cup (240 ml) half-and-half, at room temperature

1 to 2 tsp (5 to 10 ml) medium-dry or dry sherry, optional

DUMPLINGS

1 cup (120 g) all-purpose flour

2 tbsp (18 g) cornmeal

1 ½ tsp (7 g) baking powder

¼ tsp baking soda

½ tsp salt

Freshly ground black pepper, to taste

3 tbsp (45 ml) butter, melted and slightly cooled

⅓ cup (71 ml) buttermilk, at room temperature

2 tbsp (6 g) fresh minced parsley, divided

In a large, deep pot or Dutch oven over medium-high heat, melt the butter and vegetable oil. Generously season all sides of the chicken with the House Seasoning. Brown the chicken on all sides, working in batches so as to not crowd the pot, about 4 to 6 minutes per side, and adding more butter and oil as necessary. Transfer the chicken to a large slow cooker. Top the chicken with the carrots, celery, garlic, thyme and bay leaves. Pour the chicken broth over the contents of the slow cooker, cover the slow cooker and cook on low for 6 hours.

Prepare the dumpling dough by whisking together the flour, cornmeal, baking powder, baking soda, salt and pepper in a medium bowl. Stir in the melted butter, buttermilk and 1 tablespoon (3 g) parsley until just combined.

In a medium bowl, combine the flour and half-and-half until smooth. Transfer the chicken to a cutting board and stir the half-and-half mixture into the slow cooker. Cover the slow cooker and increase the heat to high. Remove the skin, bones and any cartilage from the chicken and discard them. Pull the chicken into bite-size chunks and return it to the slow cooker. Stir in the sherry and remaining 1 tablespoon (3 g) parsley. Adjust the seasonings with additional salt and pepper, if desired.

Drop rustic, tablespoon-size dumplings into the slow cooker, first in a ring around the outer edge and then toward the center. Cover the slow cooker and cook on high for 1 to 1 ½ hours, until the dumplings are fluffy and fully cooked through. Discard the bay leaves and gently stir to break apart the dumplings before serving.

# TEX-MEX CREAMY CORN CHOWDER

Once upon a time, I decided to take one of my all-time favorite dip recipes and turn it into a thick, chunky chowder. The ingredients perfectly complemented one another, with sweet corn balanced by a touch of heat and smoky cumin countering cool sour cream. My family loved the chowder, but I selfishly hoarded the leftovers and ate it on-the-sly every day for lunch until it was all gone. They begged for more, so I vowed to make it again soon. And now I'm sharing it here for y'all to enjoy, too! *The end.*

YIELD: 6 TO 8 SERVINGS

1 to 2 medium jalapeños (seeds and membranes left intact for spicy, removed for mild)

½ cup (20 g) packed fresh cilantro leaves, plus more for serving

3 lb (1.4 kg) frozen corn, thawed, divided

4 cups (1 L) low-sodium chicken broth or vegetable broth, divided

1 ½ tbsp (10 g) ground cumin

4 tsp (16 g) House Seasoning (page 193)

¾ cup (170 g) sour cream

½ cup (60 g) all-purpose flour

1 ½ cups (6 oz [170 g]) shredded sharp cheddar cheese, plus more for serving

Salt and freshly ground black pepper, to taste

Crushed tortilla chips, for serving

Sliced fresh or pickled jalapeños, for serving

In a large food processor or blender, pulse the jalapeños and cilantro until they are minced. Add 1 ½ pounds (680 g) of the corn, 2 cups (480 ml) of the chicken or vegetable broth, the cumin and the House Seasoning. Purée the corn mixture until smooth. Transfer the mixture to a large slow cooker and stir in the remaining 1 ½ pounds (680 g) corn and the remaining 2 cups (480 ml) chicken or vegetable broth. Cover the slow cooker and cook on low for 4 hours.

Add the sour cream to a medium bowl and temper it, to prevent curdling, by adding a small amount of hot chowder to the bowl while continuously stirring the sour cream. Repeat this process several times to gradually bring up the temperature of the sour cream. Once the sour cream is warm, mix the flour into the sour cream mixture until smooth. Scrape the sour cream mixture back into the slow cooker, and stir to combine. Stir in the cheddar. Cover the slow cooker and cook on high for 30 minutes, until the chowder has thickened. Adjust the seasoning with additional salt and pepper, if desired. Garnish with additional cilantro, additional cheddar, the crushed tortilla chips and the sliced jalapeños.

# PULLED-PORK CHILI

In case you've never tried it, tender, succulent, juicy pork roast makes for one darn good chili. This version is loaded with spices, garnering the majority of its heat from chipotle chile powder. There's a decent amount added at the beginning of the recipe, but keep in mind that you're dealing with a big hunk of meat and a long cooking time, which will tone down some of that spiciness. Nevertheless, if your family prefers things mild, you can reduce the chipotle chile powder and remove the seeds and membranes from the jalapeños.

YIELD: 8 TO 10 SERVINGS

---

¼ cup (30 g) all-purpose flour

½ cup (120 ml) low-sodium chicken broth

1 (12-oz [355-ml]) bottle dark beer (see page 17 for recommendations)

4 lb (1.8 g) boneless pork butt roast, trimmed

1 ½ tbsp (18 g) House Seasoning (page 193)

2 tbsp (16 g) chili powder

1 tbsp (7 g) ground cumin

1 tbsp (5 g) unsweetened cocoa powder

2 tsp (6 g) chipotle chile powder

1 tsp (1 g) dried Mexican oregano

1 medium yellow onion, finely chopped

8 cloves garlic, minced

2 medium jalapeños, minced (seeds and membranes left intact for spicy, removed for mild)

1 (28-oz [794-g]) can fire-roasted crushed tomatoes

Salt and freshly ground black pepper, to taste

Cayenne pepper, to taste, optional

2 (15-oz [425-g]) cans black beans, drained and rinsed

1 (15-oz [425-g]) can pinto beans, drained and rinsed

Chopped fresh cilantro, for serving

Diced avocado, for serving

Sour cream, for serving

Shredded sharp cheddar cheese, for serving

Crushed tortilla chips, for serving

In a medium bowl, whisk the flour into the chicken broth until smooth and pour the mixture into the bottom of large slow cooker. Add the beer and stir to combine. Pierce the pork roast all over with a small knife. Place the pork in the slow cooker. Sprinkle it with the House Seasoning, chili powder, cumin, cocoa powder, chipotle chile powder and Mexican oregano. Top the roast with the onion, garlic, jalapeños and crushed tomatoes. Cover the slow cooker and cook on low for 8 to 10 hours, or on high for 4 to 5 hours, until the pork is tender.

Transfer the pork to a cutting board. Use a large spoon to skim the fat from the surface of the cooking liquids in the slow cooker. Shred and pull the pork into chunks, discarding any fat, and return the pulled pork to slow cooker. Combine the pork with the liquids in the slow cooker and add the salt and pepper to taste. Stir in the cayenne pepper ¼ teaspoon at a time if more heat is desired. Gently stir in the black beans and pinto beans. Cover the slow cooker and cook on low for 2 hours, or on high for 1 hour, to allow the flavors to meld. Serve the Pulled-Pork Chili piled high with the cilantro, avocado, sour cream, cheddar and tortilla chips.

# ALPHABET VEGETABLE STEW

Alphabet soup is a quintessential childhood staple. But the next time you consider cracking open that red and white can, why not try your hand at this chunky, homemade, stew-like version instead? With a variety of vegetables and two kinds of mushrooms in a thick, hearty broth, you won't even miss the meat! It's also easy to tweak this recipe to your family's tastes or to what you have available. Add a cup of chopped onion if you like. Use any type of potato that you wish. Thin-skinned red or yellow potatoes are fine unpeeled; or russets work, too, if you don't mind peeling. The mushrooms are also customizable— you can use all the same kind or mix 'em up. And finally, there's the namesake pasta. While I will warn you that alphabet-shaped pasta can sometimes be difficult to find, I promise that this stew tastes just as good with macaroni or another type of small pasta. Just bear in mind that since pasta can continue to absorb liquid even after it's cooked, you may need to add a splash of broth to the bowl when reheating any leftovers.

YIELD: 6 TO 8 SERVINGS

1 lb (454 g) red or yellow potatoes, scrubbed and cut into 1-inch (2.5-cm) pieces

6 medium carrots, peeled and cut into ½-inch (13-mm) thick slices

2 medium stalks celery, finely chopped

1 cup (135 g) frozen corn, thawed

1 cup (121 g) frozen green beans, thawed

8 oz (227 g) white mushrooms, cleaned and cut into ¼-inch (6-mm) thick slices

8 oz (227 g) cremini mushrooms, cleaned and cut into ¼-inch (6-mm) thick slices

4 cloves garlic, minced

1 (14.5-oz [411-g]) can fire-roasted crushed tomatoes

5 cups (1.2 L) low-sodium vegetable broth

1 tbsp (17 g) tomato paste

1 tbsp (15 ml) balsamic vinegar

1 tbsp (12 g) House Seasoning (page 193)

1 tbsp (3 g) Italian Seasoning (page 193)

1 tsp (2 g) chopped fresh rosemary or ¼ tsp dried rosemary

2 dried bay leaves

2 tbsp (16 g) cornstarch plus 2 tbsp (30 ml) water

1 cup (112 g) dry alphabet pasta, small elbow macaroni or any other type of small pasta

1 cup (134 g) frozen peas, thawed

Salt and freshly ground black pepper, to taste

Combine the potatoes, carrots, celery, corn, green beans, white mushrooms, cremini mushrooms, garlic and crushed tomatoes in a large slow cooker. Pour in the vegetable broth, then add the tomato paste, balsamic vinegar, House Seasoning, Italian Seasoning, rosemary and bay leaves, stirring to combine. Cover the slow cooker and cook on low for 8 hours, or on high for 4 hours, until all of the vegetables are tender.

In a small bowl, mix the cornstarch and water until smooth, then slowly stir the cornstarch slurry into the slow cooker, along with the pasta and peas. Cover the slow cooker and cook on high for 15 to 30 minutes, until the pasta is al dente. Discard the bay leaves. Adjust the seasoning to taste with salt and pepper, if desired.

### Samantha's Tip

To quickly thaw frozen vegetables, placed them in a colander and rinse them under warm running water for a minute or two.

# BEEF BOURGUIGNON

The French know how to do flavor, and they *definitely* know how to do beef stew. In this dish—which I am shamelessly unable to spell, much less pronounce—layers of flavor are built with bacon, beef and red wine. And if the resulting stew doesn't just sound good enough to drink with a straw . . . well, it is. Except that, unfortunately, all those chunks of veggies might get in the way. So be all civilized and French-like by eating it with a spoon and doing your best not to slurp, even though that's a tall order when something is this delicious. Also, be sure to use a decent wine as it's an important flavor in the final dish, and complete your meal with roasted or mashed potatoes and a big green salad!

YIELD: 6 SERVINGS

---

¾ cup (90 g) all-purpose flour

1 ½ tsp (9 g) salt, divided, plus more to taste

Freshly ground black pepper, to taste

2 ½ to 3 lb (1.1 to 1.4 kg) boneless beef chuck roast, trimmed and cut into 1 ½-inch (4-cm) cubes

8 slices bacon, cut into ½-inch (13-mm) pieces (about 8 oz [227 g])

1 tbsp (15 ml) vegetable oil, plus more as needed

2 ½ cups (600 ml) dry red wine (such as Burgundy, Côtes du Rhône, Beaujolais or Pinot Noir)

1 cup (240 ml) low-sodium beef broth

6 medium carrots, peeled and cut diagonally into 1-inch (2.5-cm) thick slices

8 oz (227 g) white mushrooms, cleaned and cut into ¼-inch (6-mm) thick slices

6 cloves garlic, minced

1 tbsp (2 g) dried parsley

½ tsp dried thyme

1 dried bay leaf

2 tbsp (16 g) cornstarch plus 2 tbsp (30 ml) water

8 oz (225 g) frozen pearl onions, thawed

In a large plastic zip-top bag, combine the flour, 1 teaspoon (6 g) of the salt and a generous amount of black pepper. Add the beef cubes to the bag and shake to coat them with the flour mixture and set aside. In a large pot or Dutch oven, cook the chopped bacon over medium-high heat until it is crispy. With a slotted spoon, transfer the bacon to a paper towel–lined plate to drain, leaving the remaining bacon grease in the pot.

Scoop the beef out of the bag, shaking off any excess flour and transfer the beef to the pot in a single layer. Working in batches so as not to crowd the pot, cook the beef until it is browned on all sides. If the meat absorbs all of the bacon grease at any point, add the vegetable oil to the pot to finish browning the beef, repeating as necessary. Use a slotted spoon to transfer the browned beef to the slow cooker.

Remove the pot from the heat and add the red wine and beef broth. Return the pot to the stove and bring the wine-broth mixture to a boil over medium-high heat for about 1 minute, scraping the bottom of the pot with a wooden spoon to deglaze the brown bits. Remove the pot from the heat and set aside to slightly cool.

Add the bacon, carrots, mushrooms, garlic, parsley and thyme to the slow cooker. Pour in the wine-broth mixture. Stir in the remaining ½ teaspoon salt, a generous amount of freshly ground black pepper and the bay leaf. Cover the slow cooker and cook on low for 7 to 9 hours, or on high for 3 ½ to 4 ½ hours, until the beef is tender.

Discard the bay leaf. In a small bowl, mix the cornstarch and the water until smooth, then slowly stir the cornstarch slurry into the slow cooker. Stir in the pearl onions, cover the slow cooker, and cook on high for 30 minutes, until the stew is thickened and heated through. Season the dish to taste with additional salt and pepper and serve immediately.

# DADDY'S TEXAS CHILI

Every good Texan knows that true Texas chili does not start with ground beef, and it does not (*gasp!*) contain beans. Despite being born in Los Angeles, my daddy grew up in Texas and, even after traveling the world for thirty-two years in the Navy, he always identified himself as a Texan. This simple chili is a slow cooker adaptation of his recipe, and the fact that my brother has used it to enter (and win!) chili cook-offs in other states just goes to show that you don't have to be from the Lone Star State to appreciate a Texas classic. And speaking of winning, adding the spices in stages at the beginning and end of this particular recipe is an old chili cook-off trick that builds layer of flavor.

YIELD: 4 TO 6 SERVINGS

2 ½ lb (1.1 kg) boneless beef chuck roast, trimmed and cut into 1-inch (2.5-cm) cubes

Salt and freshly ground black pepper, to taste

2 tbsp (30 ml) vegetable oil, plus more as needed

1 medium yellow onion, finely chopped

6 cloves garlic, minced

3 (14.5-oz [411-g]) cans fire-roasted diced tomatoes, drained

1 to 2 medium jalapeños, minced (seeds and membranes left intact for spicy, removed for mild)

3 tbsp (24 g) chili powder, divided

2 tbsp (24 g) House Seasoning (page 193), divided

2 tsp (5 g) ground cumin, divided

2 tsp (2 g) dried Mexican oregano, divided

1 tsp (3 g) ground coriander, divided

1 (12-oz [355-ml]) bottle dark beer (see page 17 for recommendations)

¼ cup (29 g) masa harina (Mexican corn flour) plus ½ cup (120 ml) water

¼ tsp cayenne pepper, plus more to taste, optional

Generously season the beef cubes on all sides with salt and pepper to taste. Heat the oil in a large pot or Dutch oven over medium-high heat until it is shimmering. Working in batches so as not to crowd the pot, add a single layer of beef cubes and cook until they are browned, about 2 to 3 minutes per side. Transfer the browned beef to a large slow cooker.

Add a bit more oil to the pot along with the onion and garlic. Cook, stirring occasionally, for 5 to 7 minutes, until the onion has softened. Transfer the onion and garlic to the slow cooker.

Add the diced tomatoes, jalapeños and 1 ½ tablespoons (12 g) of the chili powder, 1 tablespoon (12 g) of the House Seasoning, 1 teaspoon (2 g) of the cumin, 1 teaspoon (1 g) of the Mexican oregano and ½ teaspoon of the coriander to the slow cooker. Slowly pour in the beer and stir to combine all of the contents of the slow cooker. Cover the slow cooker and cook on low for 7 to 9 hours, or on high for 3 ½ to 4 ½ hours.

In a small bowl, mix the masa with the water until dissolved. Stir the masa mixture into the chili, along with remaining 1 ½ tablespoons (12 g) chili powder, the remaining 1 tablespoon (12 g) House Seasoning, the remaining 1 teaspoon (2 g) cumin, the remaining 1 teaspoon (1 g) Mexican oregano, the remaining ½ teaspoon coriander and the cayenne pepper (if using). Increase the heat to high, cover the slow cooker and cook for 15 to 30 minutes, until the chili is thickened. (If even thicker chili is desired, remove the lid of the slow cooker and continue to cook for 15 to 30 more minutes to allow excess liquid to evaporate.)

# SWEET POTATO AND BLACK BEAN CHILI

I have always been a sweet and savory kind of gal. Bacon dipped in maple syrup? *Love it.* Salty ham and luscious pineapple atop a Hawaiian pizza? *My favorite.* Frosty frozen margarita with a salted rim? *I'll take two.* So it should come as no surprise that this chili, loaded with (sweet!) sweet potatoes and (savory!) black beans, is the stuff of dreams. And on top of its delicious flavor combo, it happens to be healthy, hearty and filling! Alas, bacon and maple syrup can't say the same.

### YIELD: 4 TO 6 SERVINGS

1 lb (454 g) sweet potatoes, peeled and cut into ¾-inch (19-mm) cubes

1 medium red bell pepper, seeded and finely chopped

½ medium yellow onion, finely chopped

6 cloves garlic, minced

2 (15-oz [425-g]) cans black beans, drained and rinsed

1 (14.5-oz [411-g]) can fire-roasted diced tomatoes

2 ½ cups (600 ml) low-sodium vegetable broth or chicken broth

2 tbsp (16 g) chili powder

1 tbsp (7 g) ground cumin

1 tbsp (12 g) House Seasoning (page 193)

1 tsp (1 g) dried Mexican oregano

1 ½ tsp (3 g) unsweetened cocoa powder

½ tsp chipotle chile powder (more or less, to taste)

Salt and freshly ground black pepper, to taste

Sour cream, for serving

Diced avocado, for serving

In a large slow cooker, combine the sweet potatoes, bell pepper, onion, garlic, black beans, diced tomatoes, vegetable broth or chicken broth, chili powder, cumin, House Seasoning, Mexican oregano, cocoa powder and chipotle chile powder. Cover the slow cooker and cook on low for 6 to 8 hours, or on high for 3 to 4 hours, until the sweet potatoes are tender. Adjust the seasoning by adding additional salt, pepper or chipotle chile powder, if desired. Serve the Sweet Potato and Black Bean Chili topped with a dollop of the sour cream and the diced avocado.

# CREAMY CLAM CHOWDER

A big bowl of my classic Creamy Clam Chowder will give you the urge to wrap up in a thick blanket and cozy up by the fire. It's both decadent and comforting, but best of all, this version is easy to make. Diced potatoes lend it body while creamy half-and-half and a healthy dose of bacon add richness. The clams are stirred in toward the end of the cooking time to ensure that they stay tender, and a cornstarch slurry thickens up the briny broth into something truly luxurious. For an extra-special presentation, you can even serve your chowder in bread bowls!

YIELD: 6 TO 8 SERVINGS

6 slices bacon (about 6 oz [170 g] total)

1 ½ lb (683 g) yellow potatoes, peeled and cut into ½-inch (13-mm) pieces

3 cloves garlic, minced

2 (8-oz [227-ml]) bottles clam juice

2 ½ cup (600 ml) low-sodium chicken broth

1 tbsp (15 ml) freshly squeezed lemon juice

1 tsp (4 g) House Seasoning (page 193)

½ tsp dried thyme

1 dried bay leaf

3 (6 ½-oz [184-g]) cans chopped clams, undrained

1 cup (240 ml) half-and-half

¼ cup (32 g) cornstarch plus ¼ cup (60 ml) water

Minced fresh parsley, for serving

Oyster crackers and/or bread bowls, for serving

Cook the bacon (in the oven or in a skillet) until crispy. Reserve 1 tablespoon (15ml) of bacon grease and discard the rest. Drain the bacon on a paper towel-lined plate and chop. Place the potatoes, garlic and ⅔ of the chopped bacon in a large slow cooker. Cover and refrigerate the remaining bacon. Add the clam juice, chicken broth, lemon juice, reserved bacon grease, House Seasoning, dried thyme and bay leaf to the slow cooker; stir all of the ingredients to combine. Cover and cook on low for 8 to 10 hours, or high for 4 to 5 hours.

Stir the undrained clams and the half and half into the slow cooker. In a small bowl, mix cornstarch and water until smooth, then slowly stir the cornstarch slurry into the slow cooker. Cover and cook on high for 30 to 45 minutes until the chowder is slightly thickened. Garnish with the reserved reheated bacon and the minced parsley, and either serve the chowder with oyster crackers on the side or ladle it into bread bowls.

# BEEF AND BARLEY STEW

What could be better than coming home at the end of a long, chilly day to a slow cooker full of bubbling beef stew? Well, I'll tell you what: adding a surprise ingredient to that stew to change things up from your typical meat-and-potatoes dish! In this recipe, "superfood" barley provides that surprise, adding vitamins and fiber to an already-hearty base of beef and mushrooms. That's right, friends—you can actually feel virtuous enjoying this stick-to-your-ribs supper.

YIELD: 4 TO 6 SERVINGS

2 lb (910 g) boneless beef chuck roast, trimmed and cut into 1 ½-inch (4-cm) cubes

5 cloves garlic, minced

2 tsp (8 g) House Seasoning (page 193)

1 tsp (1 g) dried thyme

½ tsp dried oregano

½ tsp dried rosemary

Freshly ground black pepper, to taste

9 medium carrots, peeled and cut diagonally into ½-inch (13-mm) thick slices

8 oz (227 g) white mushrooms, cleaned and cut into ¼-inch (6-mm) thick slices

2 tbsp (33 g) tomato paste

1 tbsp (15 ml) red wine vinegar

1 tbsp (15 ml) Worcestershire sauce

¾ cup (138 g) pearl barley, rinsed and drained

2 dried bay leaves

6 cups (1.4 L) low-sodium beef broth

2 tbsp (16 g) cornstarch plus 2 tbsp (30 ml) water

Minced fresh parsley, for serving

Place the beef cubes in the bottom of a large slow cooker. Sprinkle them with the garlic, House Seasoning, thyme, oregano, rosemary and pepper and toss to coat them. Top the seasoned beef cubes with the carrots, mushrooms, tomato paste, red wine vinegar, Worcestershire sauce, barley and bay leaves. Pour the beef broth into the slow cooker and stir to combine. Cover the slow cooker and cook on low for 7 to 9 hours, or on high for 3 ½ to 4 ½ hours, until the beef is tender.

In a small bowl, mix the cornstarch and water until smooth, then slowly stir the cornstarch slurry into the slow cooker. Cover the slow cooker and cook on high for 15 to 30 minutes, until the stew is slightly thickened. Discard the bay leaves and garnish the stew with the parsley.

# IRISH LAMB AND POTATO STEW

Whether you're a fan of lamb or you're simply on the hunt for a Saint Patrick's Day–appropriate recipe, you can't get much more Irish than lamb, potatoes and Irish stout! If you don't care for lamb, however, this simple stew is also tasty when made with beef. If you can't find lamb stew meat, simply buy a 2-pound (910-g) boneless lamb shoulder and cut it into 1 ½-inch (4-cm) cubes.

YIELD: 4 TO 6 SERVINGS

2 lb (910 g) boneless lamb stew meat

2 lb (910 g) russet potatoes, peeled and cut into 1-inch (2.5-cm) cubes

1 medium yellow onion, finely chopped

4 cloves garlic, minced

1 tbsp (12 g) House Seasoning (page 193)

1 tsp (1 g) dried thyme

½ tsp dried rosemary

2 dried bay leaves

2 tbsp (33 g) tomato paste

3 cups (720 ml) low-sodium beef broth

1 cup (240 ml) Irish stout, like Guinness

2 tbsp (16 g) cornstarch plus 2 tbsp (30 ml) water

Salt and freshly ground black pepper, to taste

Combine the lamb cubes, potatoes, onion, garlic, House Seasoning, thyme, rosemary, bay leaves, tomato paste and beef broth in a large slow cooker. Slowly add the beer and gently stir to combine. Cover the slow cooker and cook on low for 8 hours, or on high for 4 hours, until the lamb and potatoes are tender.

In a small bowl, mix the cornstarch and water until smooth, then slowly stir the cornstarch slurry into the slow cooker. Cover the slow cooker and cook on high for 15 to 30 minutes, until the stew is slightly thickened. Discard the bay leaves and adjust the seasoning to taste with salt and pepper.

# SANDWICHES, TACOS AND WRAPS

## Sixteen Tasty Fillings from the Slow Cooker

Slow cookers are ideal for whipping up a variety of savory fillings for sandwiches, tacos, wraps and more! Simply throw in a big hunk of meat to braise for hours until it's fall-apart tender, all the while soaking up amazing flavor. Then slice, pull or shred that meat; pile it on the appropriate bread, bun or tortilla; top it with contrasting flavors and textures, and you're ready to enjoy a glorious, handheld supper!

If you're a sandwich aficionado, you first must decide between beef, chicken or pork. Do Asian Beef Sandwiches with ginger-infused Broccoli Slaw (page 142) sound tempting? Or perhaps you're in the type of spicy-sweet mood that only Raspberry-Chipotle Chicken Sliders (page 138) can satisfy. On the other hand, a zesty Cuban Pulled-Pork Panini (page 145) will have you doing the mambo while you wash the dinner dishes.

Maybe tacos are more your speed. French Dip Tacos with Caramelized Onions and Blue Cheese (page 158) are as flavorful as they sound. Tacos al Pastor (page 141) boast an undertone of heat that's perfectly balanced by fresh, sweet pineapple. And Chipotle Shrimp Tacos with creamy Cilantro-Lime Slaw (page 154) are the closest your slow cooker can bring you to beachside dining in Cabo.

But don't think the slow cooker limits you to just sandwiches and tacos. Tortilla wraps, lettuce wraps, gyros, mini pizzas—this chapter has it all!

# RASPBERRY-CHIPOTLE CHICKEN SLIDERS

I first discovered the wonder that is bottled raspberry-chipotle sauce as a young newlywed. It was divine over cream cheese (or Brie, *if* we got paid that week) that we then scooped up with crackers, and it was as easy as pouring it out on a plate. In fact, it became my go-to appetizer any time we hosted a shindig or attended a get-together during those years.

Well, time passed and I all but forgot about that sweet, spicy and smoky sauce that was so tasty on so many things. *Until now.* And when I recently decided to re-create its amazingness, it definitely took some trial and error. I quickly learned that if I got the balance of sweet, spicy and smoky just right from the get-go, all of those flavors became muted as the sauce cooked with the chicken in the slow cooker. But when I initially made the sauce a bit *too* spicy, it was perfect by the time it was finished cooking. If the flavors in your sauce still need a little tweaking after the chicken is done, it's not too late! Simply make a few adjustments before you thicken the sauce on the stove. The resulting pulled chicken sliders—dripping with raspberry-chipotle sauce and perfectly balanced by slices of salty, creamy Brie—put yesteryear's cream cheese and crackers to shame.

YIELD: 4 TO 6 SERVINGS

2 lb (910 g) boneless, skinless chicken breasts or thighs, trimmed

1 ½ cups (16 oz [454 g]) raspberry jam or preserves

1 ½ tbsp (23 g) adobo sauce, plus more as needed

1 large jalapeño, minced, plus more as needed

2 tbsp (30 ml) apple cider vinegar

1 tbsp (15 ml) lemon juice

Salt and freshly ground black pepper, to taste

Honey, as needed

2 tbsp (16 g) cornstarch plus 2 tbsp (30 ml) water

12 slider buns, for serving

8 oz (227 g) Brie (or another salty white cheese), sliced, for serving

Place the chicken in the bottom of a large slow cooker. In a large bowl, combine the raspberry jam, adobo sauce, jalapeño, apple cider vinegar and lemon juice. Pour the jam mixture over the chicken. Cover the slow cooker and cook on low for 3 to 5 hours, until the chicken is tender and cooked through but not dry.

Turn off the slow cooker, transfer the chicken to a plate, and use 2 forks to shred it or pull it into chunks depending on your preferred consistency. Pour the raspberry-chipotle sauce from the slow cooker into a medium saucepan and transfer the chicken back to the slow cooker. Season the chicken to taste with salt and pepper, and cover the slow cooker to keep the chicken warm.

Taste the raspberry-chipotle sauce and decide if the flavors need adjusting. If you'd like it to be sweeter, add a squeeze of honey. If you'd like it to be spicier, add more jalapeño. If you'd like it to be smokier *and* spicier, add more adobo sauce.

In a small bowl, mix the cornstarch and the water until smooth and set aside. Place the saucepan of raspberry-chipotle sauce over medium-high heat and bring to a boil. Whisk the sauce continuously while slowly pouring in the cornstarch slurry. Reduce the heat to a simmer and cook for 1 to 2 minutes, stirring constantly, until the sauce is thick and glossy. Pour the desired amount of sauce over the shredded chicken in the slow cooker and stir to combine. Serve the chicken on slider buns topped with slices of Brie, with leftover sauce drizzled on top or used as a dipping sauce.

# TACOS AL PASTOR

Ah, the glorious combination of pork and pineapple! This slow cooker version is not only a cinch to throw together, but it's sweet and savory with a touch of smoky heat at the back of your throat from the chipotle chile powder. If you have time, I highly recommend caramelizing the reserved pineapple tidbits in a saucepan to add that extra-special touch to your tacos. On the other hand, if you're short on time, this is a great recipe to prep the night before, so that all you have to do in the morning is pop everything in the slow cooker. You can trim and pierce the pork roast, as well as purée the pineapple sauce, in the evening. Store them separately in the refrigerator overnight and then in the morning, simply place the pork in the slow cooker and pour the sauce over the top. *Shazam!* Dinner is underway and it only required two minutes of your morning routine.

YIELD: 8 SERVINGS

4 to 5 lb (1.8 to 2.3 kg) boneless pork butt roast, trimmed

6 cloves garlic

¾ cup (30 g) packed fresh cilantro leaves, plus more for serving

1 medium pineapple, peeled, cored and quartered, divided

3 tbsp (45 ml) freshly squeezed orange juice

3 tbsp (45 ml) freshly squeezed lime juice

2 tbsp (30 ml) apple cider vinegar

1 ½ tbsp (18 g) House Seasoning (page 193)

1 tbsp (8 g) chili powder

1 tbsp (8 g) chipotle chile powder, plus more to taste

2 tsp (5 g) ground cumin

1 tsp (1 g) dried Mexican oregano

¾ cup (6 oz [180 ml]) dark beer (see page 17 for recommendations)

Salt and freshly ground black pepper, to taste

Cayenne pepper, to taste, optional

1 tbsp (14 g) butter, plus more as needed

12 to 16 (8-inch [20-cm]) flour tortillas, for serving

Sliced onion, for serving

Lime wedges, for serving

Pierce the pork roast all over with a small knife. Place the pork in the bottom of a large slow cooker. In a blender or large food processor, pulse the garlic until chopped. Add the cilantro leaves and pulse until minced. Add 3 of the pineapple quarters, all of the orange juice, lime juice, apple cider vinegar, House Seasoning, chili powder, chipotle chile powder, cumin and Mexican oregano and purée until the mixture is smooth. Pour the purée over the top of the pork roast. Pour the beer into the bottom of the slow cooker. Cover the slow cooker and cook on low for 8 to 10 hours, or on high for 4 to 5 hours, until the pork is very tender.

Transfer the pork to a cutting board. Remove and discard the fat and use 2 forks to pull the pork into chunks. Use a large spoon to skim the fat from the surface of the liquids in the slow cooker. Return the pulled pork to the slow cooker and stir to help it soak up the juices. Taste the meat and adjust the seasoning, adding more salt and pepper, chipotle chile powder or cayenne (if using). Cover the slow cooker and cook on high for 15 to 30 minutes, so that the pork can further absorb the flavors of the cooking liquids.

While the pork is reheating, slice the remaining quarter of the pineapple into small chunks. Heat the butter in a medium skillet over medium heat. Add the pineapple chunks and sauté them until they are golden brown and caramelized. Use a slotted spoon to load the tortillas with pork, then top the pork with the sautéed pineapple chunks, additional cilantro, sliced onions and a squeeze of lime.

# ASIAN BEEF SANDWICHES

This recipe is a sandwich-like spin on one of my favorite Chinese restaurant menu items: beef and broccoli! The tender shredded beef is positively bursting with Asian flavor, but in my humble opinion, it's the tangy slaw that sends these sandwiches over the top. Broccoli slaw is basically just shredded broccoli stalks to replace the cabbage found in traditional coleslaw, and you can find bags of it in the produce section of most grocery stores. Dressed with a mouthwatering Asian dressing, this Broccoli Slaw contributes a fabulous contrasting texture to the soft, juicy beef. If you want your slaw to be extra crunchy, don't prepare it too far ahead of time—the broccoli will soften with time as it macerates in the dressing in the refrigerator. However, that's not necessarily a bad thing, because it also becomes more infused with flavor as it soaks! And while leftovers are unlikely, the beef will continue to soak up the sauce as it chills, so you may need to splash in a little extra beef broth when reheating.

YIELD: 6 TO 8 SERVINGS

### BEEF

3 lb (1.4 kg) boneless beef chuck roast, trimmed

¾ cup (180 ml) low-sodium beef broth

3 tbsp (54 g) oyster sauce (preferably MSG-free)

3 tbsp (45 ml) honey

2 tbsp (30 ml) low-sodium soy sauce

1 ½ tsp (8 ml) rice vinegar

2 tbsp (19 g) minced fresh ginger

3 cloves garlic, minced

¼ tsp crushed red pepper flakes

½ tsp sesame oil or toasted sesame oil

Sandwich buns, for serving (make sure they're not too soft, or the juices from the beef may soak through)

### BROCCOLI SLAW

2 tbsp (30 ml) canola oil or other light vegetable oil

2 tbsp (30 ml) rice vinegar

2 tbsp (30 ml) honey

1 tbsp (15 ml) low-sodium soy sauce

½ tsp sesame oil or toasted sesame oil

1 tsp (3 g) minced fresh ginger

1 (12-oz [340-g]) bag broccoli slaw

¼ cup (30 g) sliced almonds, toasted

Place the chuck roast in the bottom of a large slow cooker. In a medium bowl, whisk together the beef broth, oyster sauce, honey, soy sauce, rice vinegar, ginger, garlic and crushed red pepper flakes. Pour the broth mixture over the roast, cover the slow cooker and cook on low for 8 to 10 hours, or on high for 4 to 5 hours.

While the roast is cooking, prepare the Broccoli Slaw. In a large bowl, whisk together the canola oil, rice vinegar, honey, soy sauce, sesame oil and minced ginger until well blended. Add the broccoli slaw and almonds and toss to coat them. Cover the bowl and refrigerate it until ready to serve.

Transfer the roast to a cutting board, remove and discard the fat, and shred the beef. Use a large spoon to skim the fat from the surface of the liquids in the slow cooker. Return the shredded beef to the slow cooker and stir in the sesame oil. Cover the slow cooker and cook on low for 1 hour, or on high for 30 minutes, so that the beef can further absorb the flavors of the sauce. Use a slotted spoon to place the shredded beef onto buns. Stir the Broccoli Slaw and use a slotted spoon to pile it on top of the beef.

# CUBAN PULLED-PORK PANINIS

Cuban pulled pork—or *lechon asado*—meets traditional Cuban ham and Swiss sandwiches in these zesty, melty paninis. The pork absorbs loads of flavor while slow cooking in a garlic- and citrus-infused *mojo* sauce, which ultimately makes for one amazing hot sandwich. Unless you live in south Florida, Cuban bread will probably be rather difficult to come by. So use whatever type of bread tickles your fancy, and if you can't find a loaf that measures 2 feet (61 cm) long, two smaller loaves (about 12 ounces [340 g] each) of Italian or French bread, or even individual hoagie rolls, would work beautifully instead. Just make sure to start and end your sandwich layers with Swiss, since the cheese is what ends up holding together an otherwise messy panini.

YIELD: 6 TO 8 SERVINGS

3 lb (1.6 kg) boneless pork butt roast, trimmed

10 cloves garlic, minced

½ cup (120 ml) freshly squeezed orange juice

¼ cup (60 ml) freshly squeezed lime juice

2 tbsp (30 ml) extra-virgin olive oil

1 tbsp (3 g) dried oregano

2 tsp (5 g) ground cumin

½ tbsp (18 g) House Seasoning (page 193)

Salt and freshly ground black pepper, to taste

1 (2-foot [61-cm] long) Cuban bread loaf, submarine sandwich roll, Italian bread loaf or French bread loaf

Prepared yellow mustard, as needed

2 (8-oz [227-g]) packages sliced Swiss cheese, divided

2 cups (286 g) sliced dill pickles

1 (8-oz [227-g]) package thinly sliced ham

4 tbsp (60 ml) melted butter

Pierce the pork roast all over with a small knife. Place the pork in the bottom of a large slow cooker. In a medium bowl, combine the garlic, orange juice, lime juice, olive oil, oregano, cumin and House Seasoning. Pour the mixture over the pork and rub it into the meat, turning to evenly coat it. Cover the slow cooker and cook on low for 8 to 10 hours, or on high for 4 to 6 hours, until the pork is extremely tender.

Transfer the pork to a cutting board. Remove and discard the fat and use 2 forks to pull the pork into chunks. Use a large spoon to skim the fat from the surface of the liquids in the slow cooker. Return the pulled pork to the slow cooker and stir well. Taste the meat and adjust the seasoning, adding salt and pepper, if desired. Cover the slow cooker and cook on high for 15 to 30 minutes, so that the pork can further absorb the flavors of the cooking liquids while you prepare the sandwich ingredients.

To assemble the sandwich, slice the loaf of bread in half horizontally. Spread a thin layer of mustard on the bottom half of the bread and then layer 1 package of the Swiss cheese, all of the pickle slices, all of the ham slices and a generous amount of pulled pork. Top the pork with the remaining 1 package of Swiss cheese and place the other half of the bread loaf on top of the Swiss cheese.

Use a serrated knife to cut the loaf into approximately 6-inch (15-cm) lengths. Brush both sides of each sandwich with the melted butter and cook the sandwiches in a panini press or a hot skillet until the cheese melts and the exterior gets toasty. If you are cooking the sandwich in a hot skillet, cover the top of the sandwich with aluminum foil and place a heavy pot or cast iron skillet on top of the foil. Flip the sandwich once the bottom is toasted and toast the other side. Cut the sandwich into slices and serve hot.

# BEEF BRISKET SANDWICHES

Right after chili, smoked beef brisket could easily be the state food of Texas. In all honesty, I was a little hesitant to attempt brisket in the slow cooker because, with such a different cooking method, it's obviously not going to turn out identical to true Texas brisket (and my father-in-law makes some of the best, so I've got a lot to live up to here). However, this brisket is pretty darn delicious in its own right. It starts with a smoked paprika–laced dry rub, which infuses the meat with some of that smoky flavor typically achieved by, well, smoking. And while authentic Texas brisket is so juicy and flavorful that eating it with barbecue sauce is practically an insult to the pit master, this version cooks in a tangy sauce that later gets drizzled over brisket sandwiches. Texas brisket is always served with dill pickle slices and raw onions, so those are layered on the sandwich as well. The only thing missing is the plain white sandwich bread synonymous with a spread of Texas barbecue. But I'm afraid it wouldn't hold up to these hearty sandwiches; hence, the sandwich buns instead. If you think you'd enjoy chopped brisket sandwiches, you can even chop up your brisket, instead of slicing it, and stir in the barbecue sauce, instead of pouring it on top. At the end of the day, this is a great recipe for when you're craving easy, tasty brisket without having to watch the pit all day. And would you believe it? It even got two thumbs-up from my father-in-law.

YIELD: 6 TO 8 SERVINGS

BRISKET DRY RUB AND BEEF

2 tbsp (26 g) brown sugar

2 tbsp (16 g) chili powder

2 tsp (7 g) garlic powder

2 tsp (4 g) smoked paprika

1 tsp (2 g) onion powder

¾ tsp mustard powder

¾ tsp salt

½ tsp freshly ground black pepper

3 to 4 lb (1.4 to 1.8 kg) beef brisket, trimmed (a thin layer of fat on top is okay)

BARBECUE SAUCE

½ cup (126 g) tomato sauce

¼ cup (60 ml) low-sodium beef broth

2 tbsp (33 g) tomato paste

2 tbsp (30 ml) molasses

2 tbsp (30 ml) apple cider vinegar

1 tsp (5 ml) Worcestershire sauce

1 tbsp (14 g) butter

Sandwich buns, for serving

Sliced pickles, for serving

Sliced onion, for serving

In a small bowl, combine the brown sugar, chili powder, garlic powder, smoked paprika, onion powder, mustard powder, salt and pepper. Coat the brisket with the dry rub, rubbing it into the meat. Wrap the brisket in plastic wrap, set it in a baking dish and refrigerate it overnight.

In the morning, place the brisket in the bottom of large slow cooker, fat-side up. In a medium bowl, whisk together the tomato sauce, beef broth, tomato paste, molasses, apple cider vinegar and Worcestershire sauce. Pour the sauce over the brisket. Cover the slow cooker and cook on low for 8 to 10 hours, or on high for 4 to 5 hours, until the brisket is tender.

Transfer the brisket to a cutting board, tent it with aluminum foil and allow it to rest for at least 20 minutes before thinly slicing it against the grain. In the meantime, use a large spoon to skim the fat from the surface of the sauce in the slow cooker and transfer the sauce to a small saucepan over medium-high heat. Bring the sauce to a boil and then reduce to a simmer. Cook the sauce until it has thickened and reduced, about 15 to 20 minutes, stirring occasionally. Stir in the butter until it has melted and, if desired, add salt and pepper to taste.

Serve the sliced brisket on sandwich buns, drizzled with the barbecue sauce and topped with sliced pickles and onions.

# MINI PULLED-PORK PIZZAS

Savory homemade pizza sauce replaces your typical barbecue sauce in this succulent spin on pulled pork. With the pork piled high on toasted English muffin halves and topped with copious amounts of mozzarella, kids and adults alike will love these tasty open-faced sandwiches, a.k.a. fun-to-eat mini pizzas! Boneless country-style pork ribs, which are actually closer to pork chops than ribs, make for fabulous pulled pork, but if you can't find any in the meat case or the butcher is all out, you can absolutely use a boneless pork butt roast instead and up the cooking time accordingly. Just don't leave out the fennel seeds in the pizza sauce! Despite the fact that fennel smells like licorice, the seeds won't make the pizza sauce taste that way. Rather, they give it a distinctive pizzeria-esque flavor and aroma. Plus, if you put them in a plastic zip-top bag and crush them with the flat side of a meat mallet, you can take out some of your frustration that the butcher was out of country-style pork ribs. Take *that!*

YIELD: 6 TO 8 SERVINGS

3 ½ lb (1.6 kg) boneless country-style pork ribs, trimmed

1 (29-oz [822-g]) can tomato sauce

6 tbsp (100 g) tomato paste

1 tbsp (15 ml) honey

3 tbsp (9 g) Italian Seasoning (page 193)

1 tbsp (12 g) House Seasoning (page 193)

½ tsp fennel seeds, crushed

¼ tsp crushed red pepper flakes

8 to 10 English muffins, split in half and toasted

2 cups (8 oz [224 g]) shredded mozzarella cheese

1 cup (180 g) freshly grated Parmesan cheese

Arrange the country-style pork ribs in the bottom of a large slow cooker. In a medium bowl, combine the tomato sauce, tomato paste, honey, Italian Seasoning, House Seasoning, fennel seeds and crushed red pepper flakes. Cover the slow cooker and cook on low for 6 to 8 hours, or on high for 4 to 5 hours, until the pork is very tender.

Transfer the pork to a cutting board. Remove and discard the fat and use 2 forks to shred the meat. Use a large spoon to skim the fat from the surface of the pizza sauce in the slow cooker. Return the pulled pork to the slow cooker and stir to combine it with the sauce. Cover the slow cooker and cook on high for 15 minutes, until the mixture is heated through.

To serve, pile the pork on top of the toasted English muffin halves. Top with the mozzarella and broil for just a couple of minutes, watching carefully, until the cheese is melted and bubbly. Sprinkle the pizzas with the Parmesan.

# HAWAIIAN CHICKEN SANDWICHES

I may have grown up in Texas, but my middle name is proof enough that I was born in Hawaii. I like to think that spending the first few years of my life there instilled in me a love of the beach, an aversion to being cold and an obsession with anything and everything pineapple. In fact, a dozen years or so ago, my then-boyfriend/now-husband and I were on vacation in Maui when he proposed to me over a bottle of pineapple champagne. So I consider these tasty sandwiches—with a fresh pineapple-infused, ginger-kissed sauce mingling with tender pulled chicken—this cookbook's tribute to my birthplace. I am a Texan through and through, but a tiny piece of my heart will always belong to Hawaii.

YIELD: 6 SERVINGS

2 ½ lb (1.1 kg) boneless, skinless chicken breasts or thighs, trimmed

1 tsp (4 g) House Seasoning (page 193)

1 tsp (2 g) ground ginger

½ tsp paprika

¼ tsp smoked paprika

2 cloves garlic

2 tbsp (19 g) minced fresh ginger

3 cups (18 oz [495 g]) chopped fresh pineapple (about half of 1 large pineapple)

1 (8-oz [228-g]) can tomato sauce

3 tbsp (54 g) oyster sauce (preferably MSG-free)

3 tbsp (45 ml) honey

1 ½ tbsp (23 ml) soy sauce

1 tbsp (15 ml) rice vinegar

2 tbsp (16 g) cornstarch plus 2 tbsp (30 ml) water

Salt and freshly ground black pepper, to taste

Sandwich buns, for serving

Canned or fresh pineapple rings, for serving

Sliced provolone cheese, for serving

Place the chicken in the bottom of a large slow cooker. In a small bowl, combine the House Seasoning, ground ginger, paprika and smoked paprika. Evenly sprinkle the spice mixture over the chicken. In a blender or large food processor, pulse the garlic until it is minced. Add the fresh ginger, pineapple, tomato sauce, oyster sauce, honey, soy sauce and rice vinegar. Purée into a smooth sauce.

Pour the sauce over the chicken in the slow cooker. Cover the slow cooker and cook on low for 3 to 5 hours, until the chicken is tender and cooked through but not dry. Transfer the chicken to a cutting board. In a small bowl, mix the cornstarch and water until smooth, then stir the cornstarch slurry into the slow cooker. Use 2 forks to shred the chicken or pull it into chunks, depending on your preferred consistency, then stir it back into the sauce in the slow cooker and season to taste with salt and pepper. Cover the slow cooker and cook on high for 15 minutes to thicken the sauce and allow the chicken to soak it up. Serve the chicken piled on warm sandwich buns, topped with the pineapple rings and provolone and briefly pop under the broiler to melt the cheese, if desired.

## Samantha's Tip

If needed, 2 (8-oz [227-g]) cans pineapple tidbits in juice, drained, may be substituted for the 3 cups (18 oz [500 g]) chopped fresh pineapple. However, if it's not as sweet as fresh pineapple, you may want to add a bit more honey.

# CHICKEN GYROS WITH TZATZIKI SAUCE

In the mood for Greek? Juicy chicken—kissed with garlic, lemon and oregano—is stuffed into fluffy pita bread and slathered with my tangy homemade Tzatziki Sauce for a Mediterranean-inspired meal that will have everyone shouting, "Opa!" If you can find an English or hothouse cucumber, those varieties lend themselves well to the Tzatziki Sauce. But a regular garden cucumber will work fine, too, as long as you remove all of its seeds and extract as much liquid from it as possible.

YIELD: 4 TO 6 SERVINGS

CHICKEN

2 lb (910 g) boneless, skinless chicken thighs, trimmed and cut into 1-inch (2.5-cm) cubes

3 cloves garlic, minced

2 tbsp (30 ml) freshly squeezed lemon juice

1 tbsp (15 ml) white wine vinegar

2 tsp (2 g) dried oregano

2 tsp (8 g) House Seasoning (page 193)

1 tsp (2 g) freshly grated lemon zest

TZATZIKI SAUCE

1 medium cucumber, peeled, seeded and finely chopped

1 tsp (6 g) salt

1 ½ cups (300 g) Greek yogurt

1 clove garlic, minced

1 tbsp (15 ml) extra-virgin olive oil

1 tbsp (15 ml) freshly squeezed lemon juice

2 tsp (10 ml) white wine vinegar

2 tbsp (6 g) fresh minced dill

Salt and freshly ground black pepper, to taste

Pita bread, for serving

Diced fresh tomatoes, for serving

Sliced red onion, for serving

Spread the chicken cubes in the bottom of a large slow cooker. In a small bowl, whisk together the garlic, lemon juice, white wine vinegar, oregano, House Seasoning and lemon zest. Pour the lemon juice mixture over the chicken and stir to combine. Cover the slow cooker and cook on low for 3 to 5 hours, until the chicken is cooked through. If possible, stir the chicken halfway through the cooking time to break up pieces that may be stuck together and to help the chicken cook more evenly. This step is not required, however.

While the chicken is cooking, prepare the Tzatziki Sauce by tossing the cucumber with the salt and placing it in a colander set over a bowl. After 30 minutes, drain the cucumber, firmly pressing down on the cucumber pieces in the colander until all of the water is extracted, and then transfer the cucumber to a medium bowl. Add the Greek yogurt, garlic, olive oil, lemon juice, white wine vinegar and dill. Season to taste with salt and pepper. Cover the Tzatziki Sauce and refrigerate it for at least 1 hour, preferably longer, before serving.

Use a slotted spoon to scoop the chicken into warm pita bread. Top the chicken with the tomatoes, onion slices and Tzatziki Sauce.

# CHIPOTLE SHRIMP TACOS

Tacos are always enthusiastically received at our house, but sometimes it's fun to change things up a bit from the usual beef or chicken. In this delightful seafood dish, spicy, buttery shrimp are balanced by a creamy cilantro-lime slaw and piled with crumbled Cotija cheese on warm corn tortillas. I prefer using fresh shrimp for this recipe, but if you start with frozen, make sure they're fully thawed. For extra heat, feel free to ramp up the chipotle chile powder and leave the seeds in the jalapeños for the slaw. So close your eyes, smell the salty air and pretend you're having dinner on the beach (on a regular ol' Wednesday night)!

### YIELD: 6 SERVINGS

SHRIMP

8 tbsp (1 stick [113 g]) butter, cut into 1-inch (2.5-cm) pieces

½ cup (120 ml) low-sodium chicken broth

1 tbsp (8 g) chili powder

1 ½ tsp (3 g) ground cumin

½ tsp chipotle chile powder

2 tsp (8 g) House Seasoning (page 193)

2 lb (910 g) large raw shrimp, peeled and deveined

CILANTRO-LIME CABBAGE SLAW

⅓ cup (76 g) Greek yogurt

1 tbsp (15 ml) freshly squeezed lime juice

1 garlic clove, minced

¼ cup (10 g) fresh cilantro leaves, minced

1 medium jalapeño, seeds and membranes removed, minced

1 tbsp (15 ml) honey, optional

Salt and freshly ground black pepper, to taste

3 cups (175 g) thinly sliced green cabbage

12 (6-inch [15-cm]) corn tortillas, for serving

Cotija cheese, for serving

Minced fresh cilantro, for serving

Lime wedges, for serving

In the bottom of a large slow cooker, combine the butter, chicken broth, chili powder, cumin, chipotle chile powder and House Seasoning. Cover the slow cooker and cook on high for 30 minutes to 1 hour to allow the butter to absorb the flavors of the spices.

In the meantime, prepare the Cilantro-Lime Cabbage Slaw by whisking together the Greek yogurt, lime juice, garlic, cilantro, jalapeño, honey (if using) and salt and pepper in the bottom of a large bowl. Add the cabbage and stir to combine. Adjust the seasoning to taste, cover the slaw and refrigerate it.

Thoroughly stir the butter mixture in the slow cooker, reduce the heat to low and add the shrimp. Toss the shrimp in the butter mixture until they are evenly coated, then cover the slow cooker and cook for 10 minutes. Stir the shrimp and cook for 10 more minutes, until the shrimp are cooked through and opaque.

Fill the corn tortillas with shrimp. Top the shrimp with the Cilantro-Lime Cabbage Slaw, crumbled Cotija, minced cilantro and a squeeze of lime juice.

# GENERAL TSO'S PULLED-PORK LETTUCE WRAPS

Sweet and spicy General Tso's sauce isn't just for the fried stuff on your favorite Chinese take-out menu—it also makes an outstanding sauce for pulled pork! In turn, this Asian-influenced pulled pork is the perfect filling for tasty little lettuce wraps. Top them with sweet carrots and sharp radishes for amazing texture and crunch. So, how many do you think you can scarf down?

YIELD: 4 TO 6 SERVINGS

2 tbsp (26 g) brown sugar

2 tsp (5 g) ground ginger

½ tsp salt

½ tsp freshly ground black pepper

⅛ tsp cayenne pepper

2 lb (910 g) boneless country-style pork ribs, trimmed

¼ cup (60 ml) water

2 cloves garlic, minced

2 tsp (6 g) grated fresh ginger

½ cup (120 ml) low-sodium chicken broth

½ cup (118 ml) honey

2 tbsp (30 ml) soy sauce

2 tbsp (30 ml) rice vinegar

1 tbsp (15 ml) sesame oil or toasted sesame oil

1 tsp to 1 tbsp (5 to 15 ml) Sriracha sauce, depending on desired heat

1 ½ tbsp (12 g) cornstarch plus 1 ½ tbsp (23 ml) water

1 medium head Bibb (butter) lettuce, leaves removed, washed and dried, for serving

Matchstick carrots, for serving

Thinly sliced radishes, for serving

In a small bowl, combine the brown sugar, ground ginger, salt, pepper and cayenne pepper. Sprinkle the pork ribs with the spice mixture and rub it into the meat.

Place the pork in a large slow cooker. Add the water to the bottom of the slow cooker. Cover the slow cooker and cook on low for 6 to 8 hours, or on high for 4 to 5 hours, until the pork is tender.

Turn off the slow cooker and transfer the pork to a cutting board. Remove and discard the fat and shred the meat. Drain the liquids from the slow cooker. Return the shredded pork to the slow cooker and cover the slow cooker to keep the meat warm.

Prepare the sauce by combining the garlic, fresh ginger, chicken broth, honey, soy sauce, rice vinegar, sesame oil and Sriracha sauce in a medium saucepan over medium-high heat. Bring the sauce to a boil. In a small bowl, mix the cornstarch and the water until smooth. Whisk the sauce continuously while slowly pouring in the cornstarch slurry. Reduce the heat to a simmer and cook for 1 to 2 minutes, stirring constantly, until the sauce is thick and glossy. Stir the sauce into the shredded pork.

To serve, scoop the warm pork onto the lettuce leaves and top with the carrots and radishes.

# FRENCH DIP TACOS WITH CARAMELIZED ONIONS AND BLUE CHEESE

Back when I first started my blog, one of my earliest "popular" recipes was Slow Cooker French Dip Sandwiches. And for good reason: they're freaking delicious! Despite the fact that the amateurish photos in that post now make me cringe, the recipe remains solid gold. So, when I had a lightbulb moment to turn those sandwiches into tacos for this cookbook, I knew I could make them even better with caramelized onions and crumbled blue cheese. Trust me . . . if that French dip recipe was good before, now it's even better.

### YIELD: 6 TO 8 SERVINGS

1 large yellow onion, cut into ½-inch (13-mm) thick slices

3 lb (1.4 kg) boneless beef chuck roast, trimmed

1 tbsp (12 g) House Seasoning (page 193)

1 tsp (1 g) dried thyme

6 cloves garlic, minced

1 ½ cups (360 ml) low-sodium beef broth

1 cup (8 oz [240 ml]) dark beer (see page 17 for recommendations)

2 tbsp (30 ml) Worcestershire sauce

Salt and freshly ground black pepper, to taste

10 to 12 (8-inch [20-cm]) flour tortillas, for serving

6 oz (170 g) crumbled blue cheese, for serving

Put the onions in the bottom of a large slow cooker and place the roast on top. Sprinkle the roast with the House Seasoning and thyme. Add the garlic, beef broth, beer and Worcestershire sauce to the slow cooker. Cover the slow cooker and cook on low for 8 to 10 hours, or on high for 4 to 5 hours, until the beef is tender.

Transfer the roast to a cutting board, remove and discard the fat, and shred the beef. Use a large spoon to skim the fat from the surface of the liquids in the slow cooker and then stir the shredded beef back into the liquids, mixing the beef with the onions. Generously season with salt and pepper to taste. Cover the slow cooker and cook on low for 1 hour, or on high for 30 minutes, so that the beef can further absorb the flavors of the cooking liquids.

Using a slotted spoon, scoop the meat and onion mixture onto the flour tortillas and top the tacos with the blue cheese crumbles. If desired, spoon some of the excess liquid from the slow cooker into a small bowl to use as an au jus in which to dip your tacos.

# KOREAN BARBECUE PORK WRAPS

The secret ingredient in this complex sauce is earthy, spicy, salty gochujang, a Korean fermented chile paste that adds depth of flavor to recipes. It should be easy to find gochujang at most any Asian market or in the Asian-foods aisle of a large grocery store, but if you can't find it locally, it can be ordered through online retailers. And whatever you do, don't leave off the Cucumber-Carrot Kimchi, which adds freshness and crunch to these flavorful wraps!

YIELD: 6 TO 8 SERVINGS

3 lb (1.4 kg) boneless pork butt roast, trimmed

6 cloves garlic, minced

⅔ cup (165 g) gochujang

½ cup (118 ml) honey

⅓ cup (80 ml) low-sodium soy sauce

⅓ cup (80 ml) rice vinegar

2 tbsp (23 g) peanut butter

2 tsp (10 ml) sesame oil or toasted sesame oil

1 tsp (2 g) onion powder

CUCUMBER-CARROT KIMCHI

2 small pickling cucumbers, cut in half lengthwise and sliced into ¼-inch (6-mm) thick half-circles

½ tsp salt

2 tbsp (30 ml) rice vinegar

2 tsp (10 ml) honey

1 tsp (5 g) gochujang

1 to 2 medium carrots, peeled and julienned

1 tbsp (10 g) minced fresh ginger

1 clove garlic, minced

¾ cup (190 g) tomato sauce

2 tbsp (30 ml) water

6 to 8 (10-inch [25-cm]) flour tortillas, for serving

Pierce the pork roast all over with a small knife. Place the pork in the bottom of a large slow cooker. In a medium bowl, combine the garlic, gochujang, honey, soy sauce, rice vinegar, peanut butter, sesame oil and onion powder. Measure out 1 cup (250 g) of the mixture and pour it over the pork roast, rubbing it into the meat and turning to evenly coat it. Refrigerate the remainder of the sauce. Cover the slow cooker and cook on low for 8 to 10 hours, or on high for 4 to 5 hours, until the pork is very tender.

While the pork is cooking, prepare the Cucumber-Carrot Kimchi. Toss the cucumbers with the salt and place them in a colander set over a bowl for 30 minutes. After 30 minutes, drain the cucumbers, firmly pressing down on the cucumber pieces in the colander until all of the water is extracted. In the bottom of a large bowl, combine the rice vinegar, honey and gochujang. Add the drained cucumbers as well as the carrots, ginger and garlic. Cover the bowl and refrigerate until ready to serve.

Prepare the Korean barbecue sauce by combining the refrigerated sauce with the tomato sauce and water in a medium saucepan over medium-high heat. Bring the sauce to a boil, reduce to a simmer and cook for 20 minutes, stirring occasionally, until the sauce has thickened and reduced.

Transfer the pork to a cutting board. Remove and discard the fat and use 2 forks to pull the pork into chunks. Use a large spoon to skim the fat from the surface of the liquids in the slow cooker. Return the pulled pork to the slow cooker and stir it to soak up the juices. Pour the desired amount of barbecue sauce over the pork and stir to combine. Serve the warm pork drizzled with the remaining sauce, topped with Cucumber-Carrot Kimchi and wrapped in flour tortillas.

# CHICKEN FAJITA TACOS

Enjoy the amazing flavor of grilled fajitas with a fraction of the effort! These tacos feature slices of juicy chicken with plenty of onions and a trio of bell peppers piled on top. This isn't a "fix it and forget it while you're gone all day" type of recipe, since you do have to give the onions a head start so that they have a chance to become soft and sweet, and then add the chicken and peppers later so that the chicken doesn't dry out and the peppers don't turn to complete mush. It's also important to note that the vegetables will naturally give off a *ton* of liquid as they cook. That's totally normal and easy to get around with a slotted spoon for serving. When all is said and done, just be sure to follow the golden rule of tacos: don't skimp on the garnishes!

## YIELD: 4 TO 6 SERVINGS

2 tbsp (30 ml) extra-virgin olive oil

2 tbsp (30 ml) freshly squeezed lime juice

1 tbsp (15 ml) honey

2 cloves garlic, minced

2 tbsp (16 g) chili powder

1 tbsp (12 g) House Seasoning (page 193)

2 tsp (5 g) ground cumin

1 tsp (1 g) dried Mexican oregano

½ tsp chipotle chile powder

2 lb (910 g) boneless, skinless chicken breasts or thighs

1 large yellow onion, halved and cut into ½-inch (13-mm) thick slices

1 medium green bell pepper, seeded and cut into ½-inch (13-mm) thick slices

1 medium red bell pepper, seeded and cut into ½-inch (13-mm) thick slices

1 medium yellow bell pepper, seeded and cut into ½-inch (13-mm) thick slices

Salt and freshly ground black pepper, to taste

8- to 10-inch (20- to 25-cm) flour tortillas, for serving

Salsa, for serving

Pico de gallo, for serving

Sour cream, for serving

Guacamole, for serving

Shredded cheddar, Monterey Jack, or Mexican blend cheese, for serving

Minced fresh cilantro, for serving

In a gallon-size plastic zip-top bag, combine the olive oil, lime juice, honey, garlic, chili powder, House Seasoning, cumin, Mexican oregano and chipotle chile powder. Add the chicken, turn and squeeze the bag to coat the chicken and place the bag in a baking dish in the refrigerator to marinate overnight.

Place the onions in the bottom of large slow cooker. Cover the slow cooker and cook on low for 3 hours, or on high for 1 ½ hours, stirring halfway through if possible. Lay the marinated chicken on top of the onions and scatter the bell peppers on top of the chicken. Cover the slow cooker and cook for 3 to 5 more hours on low, until the chicken is tender and cooked through but not dry. Transfer the chicken to a cutting board and stir the onions and bell peppers. Slice the chicken into strips or use 2 forks to pull it into large chunks. Season the chicken to taste with salt and pepper. To assemble a taco, lay several chicken pieces down the center of a flour tortilla and use a slotted spoon to place the peppers and onions on top. Generously top with the salsa, pico de gallo, sour cream, guacamole, cheese and cilantro, as desired.

# BRATWURST AND SAUERKRAUT SANDWICHES

Perhaps you've never made it to Oktoberfest, but never fear—now you can enjoy a (stereotypical) taste of Deutschland in your very own kitchen! From the first time I took my husband to Germany to visit my relatives there, he's been a huge fan of German food. Sausage, mustard, pretzels, beer: What's not to love? He even fell for sauerkraut. However, if sauerkraut is typically a little too *sour* for you, this recipe tempers that pungency with sweet apples, apple juice and a touch of beer. Paired with smoky, salty brats and a healthy dose of whole-grain mustard, it's like an oompah band on a sandwich!

YIELD: 8 SERVINGS

1 (24-oz [680-g]) jar sauerkraut, drained and rinsed

1 large sweet apple, peeled, cored and cut into matchsticks

1 cup (240 ml) light lager-style beer (see page 17 for recommendations)

½ cup (120 ml) unsweetened apple juice

2 tbsp (50 ml) honey, optional

½ tsp caraway seeds

½ tsp salt

Freshly ground black pepper, to taste

2 dried bay leaves

8 uncooked bratwurst links

8 sandwich rolls, for serving

Whole-grain mustard, for serving

8 slices bacon, cooked until crispy and chopped, for serving

Diced onion, for serving

In a large bowl, combine the sauerkraut, apple, beer, apple juice, honey (if using), caraway seeds, salt, pepper and bay leaves. Place half of the sauerkraut mixture in a large oval slow cooker. Arrange the bratwurst links on top. Cover the bratwurst links with the remaining sauerkraut mixture. Cover the slow cooker and cook on low for 2 to 4 hours, until the bratwurst is tender and fully cooked, reaching an internal temperature of 165°F (74°C). Discard the bay leaves. Serve the hot brats on sandwich rolls that have been spread with the whole-grain mustard, and use a slotted spoon to top the brats with the sauerkraut. Sprinkle the sauerkraut with the chopped bacon and diced onions.

# CHICKEN CAESAR SANDWICHES

Chicken Caesar Sandwiches are perfect when you're craving the flavors of a Caesar salad but in something more substantial. Moist and flavorful chicken is poached in the slow cooker and enveloped in a creamy, tangy, homemade dressing. That chicken is then piled on your choice of Italian buns with an array of obligatory Caesar salad ingredients—chopped romaine, shaved Parmesan and even crushed croutons! Of course, if you prefer to skip the bread, this Caesar-dressed chicken would also be scrumptious in wraps or even—who'd have guessed?—atop a salad.

YIELD: 4 TO 6 SERVINGS

CHICKEN

½ cup (120 ml) low-sodium chicken broth

2 lb (910 g) boneless, skinless chicken thighs, trimmed and cut into 1-inch (2.5-cm) cubes

1 tbsp (3 g) Italian Seasoning (page 193)

2 tsp (8 g) House Seasoning (page 193)

CAESAR DRESSING

1 clove garlic, minced

½ cup (90 g) freshly grated Parmesan cheese

1 tsp (6 g) anchovy paste or 2 anchovy fillets, mashed

2 tbsp (30 ml) freshly squeezed lemon juice

2 tsp (10 g) Dijon mustard

1 tsp (5 ml) red wine vinegar

½ tsp Worcestershire sauce

⅓ cup (80 ml) extra-virgin olive oil

Salt and freshly ground black pepper, to taste

Focaccia, ciabatta or Italian rolls, for serving

Chopped romaine lettuce, for serving

Crushed croutons, for serving

Shaved Parmesan cheese, for serving

Pour the chicken broth into the bottom of a large slow cooker. Spread the chicken cubes in the slow cooker and sprinkle them with the Italian Seasoning and House Seasoning, stirring to coat the chicken. Cover the slow cooker and cook on low for 3 to 5 hours, until the chicken is cooked through. If possible, stir the chicken halfway through the cooking time to break up pieces that may be stuck together and to help the chicken cook more evenly.

Just before the chicken is done, prepare the Caesar Dressing by placing the garlic, Parmesan, anchovy paste or fillets, lemon juice, Dijon mustard, red wine vinegar, Worcestershire sauce and olive oil in a blender or small food processor and purée until smooth. Season the dressing with salt and pepper to taste and set aside.

Once the chicken is cooked through, carefully stir it to break apart the cubes. Turn off the slow cooker, use a slotted spoon to remove the chicken to a bowl and gently stir in the desired amount of Caesar Dressing. Pile the warm chicken on buns and top with additional dressing (if desired), chopped romaine, crushed croutons and shaved Parmesan.

# CARNE GUISADA SOFT TACOS

Carne guisada is a Tex-Mex style beef stew that's cooked low and slow in a spicy brown gravy. And while it can certainly be eaten as a stew, we like to fold up the tender chunks of beef in soft flour tortillas. The best way to thicken up this dish in the slow cooker is to stir in a slurry of masa harina (Mexican corn flour, though you can use all-purpose flour if masa is not available) and then leave off the lid for a bit, so that some of the liquid evaporates while the masa does its magic. It's double the thickening power, which makes for a singularly mouthwatering tortilla topping!

YIELD: 6 TO 8 SERVINGS

2 lb (910 g) boneless beef chuck roast, trimmed and cut into 1 ½-inch (4-cm) cubes

1 medium yellow onion, finely chopped

1 medium green bell pepper, seeded and finely chopped

6 cloves garlic, minced

1 medium jalapeño (seeds and membranes left intact for spicy, removed for mild)

1 (14.5-oz [411-g]) can fire-roasted diced tomatoes

1 ½ cups (360 ml) low-sodium beef broth

1 ½ tbsp (18 g) House Seasoning (page 193)

1 tbsp (8 g) chili powder

1 tbsp (7 g) ground cumin

1 tsp (1 g) dried Mexican oregano

1 dried bay leaf

¼ cup (29 g) masa harina (Mexican corn flour) plus ½ cup (120 ml) water

Salt and freshly ground black pepper, to taste

Flour tortillas, for serving

Sliced avocado, for serving

Chopped onion, for serving

Minced fresh cilantro, for serving

Combine the beef cubes, onion, bell pepper, garlic, jalapeño, diced tomatoes, beef broth, House Seasoning, chili powder, cumin, Mexican oregano and bay leaf in a large slow cooker. Cover the slow cooker and cook on low for 7 hours, or on high for 3 ½ hours, until the beef is tender.

In a small bowl, mix the masa harina with the water until the masa harina is dissolved. Gently stir the masa mixture into the slow cooker, so as not to break up the chunks of beef, increase the heat to high and cook for 30 more minutes, uncovered, stirring occasionally to prevent sticking, until the sauce has thickened. Season to taste with additional salt and pepper. Scoop the beef onto the flour tortillas and top with the avocado slices, onions and cilantro.

# HOLIDAY HELPERS

## Ten Recipes to Simplify Life This Holiday Season

Pull out the slow cooker this holiday season to make your life easier—and your meals tastier! Holiday dinners mean all hands on deck, and, oftentimes, they also mean not enough oven space for the many dishes that need to be prepared at the same time. So ease the burden on your oven (and your sanity) by relying on the slow cooker for that special main dish!

In just a few hours, the slow cooker can turn out a moist, tender Herbed Turkey Breast (page 172) or a gorgeous Cran-Cherry Glazed Ham (page 175). Or for something especially festive, Citrus-Glazed Cornish Hens (page 180) are guaranteed to elicit *oohs* and *ahhs*.

There are also delicious, impressive recipes for feeding the masses of house guests that you may find yourself hosting over the holidays. Tickle their taste buds and fill their bellies with savory Holiday Pot Roast (page 176). Or wow everyone with a gorgeous Garlic "Roasted" Whole Chicken (page 184), complete with root veggies to soak up all of those mouthwatering juices.

And if you're not sure how to use up leftovers, never fear! Turkey and Wild Rice Soup (page 187) and Cheesy Potato Soup with Ham (page 188) will put that excess turkey and ham to good use while simultaneously providing a warm, comforting meal.

So don't tuck away the slow cooker over the holidays! After all, some of its best work is done when your focus is centered on making memories with loved ones.

# HERBED TURKEY BREAST

You may be hosting a small Thanksgiving dinner with too few dinner guests to justify a giant turkey, or maybe you're out of oven space. You may be intimidated about cooking a whole turkey. You may highly prefer turkey breast over dark meat. You may love turkey so much that you want to eat it all year long, even when whole raw turkeys are hard to come by. If any of these scenarios describe you, never fear! This Herbed Turkey Breast turns out juicy and flavorful every time. Switch up the herbs for whichever kinds are your favorite, as long as you use the same total amount, and don't even think about skipping out on the (easy!) homemade gravy. The one kitchen tool that I would definitely recommend for this recipe is a probe-type digital meat thermometer that can hang out in your turkey the entire time it slow cooks. Turkey breast is really easy to overcook and, depending on the thickness of your turkey breast and the power of your slow cooker, it may even be done in under three and a half hours. But the only way to know for sure, thereby avoiding dry, overcooked turkey, is to use a meat thermometer. So enjoy the star of Thanksgiving dinner any day of the year, thanks to this slow cooker wonder!

YIELD: 6 TO 8 SERVINGS

## TURKEY

6 lb (2.7 kg) bone-in, skin-on whole turkey breast

1 tbsp (12 g) House Seasoning (page 193), divided

2 tbsp (6 g) minced fresh parsley

1 tbsp (2 g) minced fresh sage

2 tsp (2 g) minced fresh thyme

4 tbsp (56 g) butter, at room temperature

Sprigs of fresh parsley, sage and thyme, as needed

1 cup (240 ml) low-sodium chicken broth

## TURKEY GRAVY

Butter, as needed

Low-sodium chicken broth, as needed

6 tbsp (45 g) all-purpose flour

Salt and freshly ground black pepper, to taste

Season the bottom of the turkey breast with 1 teaspoon (4 g) of the House Seasoning and place it in a large slow cooker, skin-side up. Mix the parsley, sage, thyme and the remaining 2 teaspoons (8 g) House Seasoning into the butter until well combined.

Slip spoonfuls of the herb butter under the turkey skin and gently smooth over the top of the skin to spread out the butter in a thin layer. Drop sprigs of parsley, sage and thyme on each side of the turkey and pour the chicken broth into the bottom of the slow cooker.

Cover the slow cooker and cook on low for 3 ½ to 6 hours, until the internal temperature of the turkey breast reaches 170°F (77°C) in multiple areas, including the thickest part of the breast. Remove the turkey to a cutting board, tent it with aluminum foil and allow it to rest for at least 20 minutes.

While the turkey breast is resting, pour the juices from the bottom of the slow cooker through a fine-mesh sieve into a large measuring cup, discarding the solids. Allow the juices to sit for 5 minutes and then use a spoon to skim any fat from the surface, transferring the fat into a medium saucepan.

There should be a total of 6 tablespoons (90 ml) fat in the saucepan; if necessary, add enough butter to make up the difference. There should be a total of 3 cups (720 ml) turkey juices in the measuring cup; if necessary, add enough chicken broth to make up the difference.

Heat the saucepan over medium-high heat until the fat-butter mixture is bubbly, and then whisk in the flour. Cook for 2 minutes while continuously whisking. Continue to whisk while slowly pouring in the turkey juices–chicken broth mixture. Bring the mixture to a boil, reduce to a simmer and cook, still whisking, for about 5 minutes or until it has thickened. Taste and adjust the seasoning with salt and pepper. Remove the saucepan from the heat and cover it to keep the gravy warm. Carve the turkey breast and serve with the Turkey Gravy.

# CRAN-CHERRY GLAZED HAM

Popping a ham in the slow cooker is an effortless way to prepare a pivotal holiday main dish, thereby trimming your meal to-do list while freeing up precious oven space. Simply start with a fully cooked ham, jazz it up with a memorable sauce and slow cook it until a safe internal temperature is reached. In the case of this ham, lightly spiced Cran-Cherry Sauce makes for a yummy and festive, sweet and tart glaze. The nice thing about this recipe is that it's fairly adaptable as far as ham size, so long as you make sure that the ham you buy will fit into your slow cooker! But for a small family or a regular weeknight meal, you can also make this recipe with a 4-pound (1.8-kg) or smaller ham, cutting the other ingredients in half and reducing the cooking time down to as little as 2 or 3 hours.

YIELD: 12 TO 16 SERVINGS

7 to 8 lb (3.2 to 3.6 kg) fully cooked bone-in or boneless ham

1 cup (240 ml) unsweetened or low-sugar cranberry juice

1 cup (10 oz [300 g]) cherry preserves

2 cups (440 g) packed dark or light brown sugar

½ tsp ground cinnamon

¼ tsp ground nutmeg

¼ tsp ground allspice

2 tbsp (30 ml) red wine vinegar

2 tbsp (16 g) cornstarch plus 2 tbsp (30 ml) water

Remove the ham from its packaging, pat it dry with paper towels and, if necessary, discard any flavor packet or plastic cap on the end of the bone. In the bottom of a large slow cooker, stir together the cranberry juice and cherry preserves. In a medium bowl, combine the brown sugar, cinnamon, nutmeg and allspice, then stir in the red wine vinegar to make a paste. Spread the brown sugar paste all over the ham and place it, flat-side down, in the slow cooker. Cover the slow cooker and cook on low for 4 to 6 hours, until the ham is tender and the internal temperature reaches 140°F (60°C). If possible, flip and baste the ham halfway through the cooking time.

Once the ham is done, transfer it to a platter and tent it with aluminum foil to keep it warm. Using a large spoon, skim any fat from the surface of the juices in the slow cooker and strain the juices through a fine-mesh sieve into a medium-sized saucepan. Heat the saucepan over medium-high heat and bring the cooking juices to a boil, stirring occasionally. In a small bowl, mix the cornstarch and the water until smooth. Whisk the glaze continuously while slowly pouring in the cornstarch slurry. Reduce the heat to a simmer and cook for a 1 to 2 minutes, stirring constantly, until the glaze is thick and glossy. Remove the saucepan from the heat and cover it to keep the glaze warm.

For an optional oven-baked effect, position an oven rack 8 inches (20 cm) below the heating element and preheat the broiler. Line a large, rimmed baking sheet with heavy-duty aluminum foil and transfer the ham to it. Broil the ham for 5 to 10 minutes, watching carefully and brushing with additional glaze every 2 minutes. Serve the ham with the glaze on the side or drizzled on top.

# HOLIDAY POT ROAST

When it comes to making pot roast on a regular ol' weeknight, I'm typically too lazy—er, *busy*—to brown the beef before throwing it in the slow cooker (and I honestly think that it still turns out fabulous regardless of skipping that step). *However*. If we're talking about an intimate meal while hosting extended family or out-of-town guests over the holidays, I feel like I should go to at least a *tiny* bit more effort in order to make things extra special. And so—in the case of easy, tasty, universally adored pot roast—I take a few extra minutes to sear the roast. And then, for good measure, I get generous with the garlic and herbs, I sub red wine for some of the beef broth and I boost the overall flavor profile with Dijon mustard. Sometimes, if I'm feeling particularly wild and crazy, I even toss in half a pound of thickly sliced mushrooms. But, *pssst*, here's a little secret: no need to wait for a special occasion. This holiday-worthy pot roast can make your family swoon tomorrow!

YIELD: 6 SERVINGS

2 lb (910 g) small yellow or red potatoes, unpeeled and left whole (or cut into chunks if using larger potatoes)

1 medium yellow onion, cut into 8 wedges

House Seasoning (page 193), to taste

3 ½ to 4 lb (1.6 to 1.8 kg) boneless beef chuck roast, trimmed

2 tbsp (30 ml) vegetable oil

1 cup (240 ml) low-sodium beef broth

1 cup (240 ml) dry red wine (such as Cabernet Sauvignon or Pinot Noir)

2 tbsp (30 ml) Worcestershire sauce

1 ½ tbsp (24 g) Dijon mustard

5 cloves garlic, minced

3 tbsp (9 g) minced fresh parsley

1 tbsp (5 g) minced fresh rosemary

1 tbsp (3 g) minced fresh thyme

1 tsp (6 g) salt, plus more to taste

Freshly ground black pepper, to taste

2 tbsp (16 g) cornstarch plus 2 tbsp (30 ml) water

1 tsp (5 ml) balsamic vinegar, optional

Combine the potatoes and onion in the bottom of a large slow cooker, and sprinkle them with the House Seasoning to taste. Pat the roast dry with paper towels and generously season both sides with the House Seasoning, rubbing it into the meat. Heat the vegetable oil in a large pot or Dutch oven over medium-high heat. Once the oil is shimmering, add the roast and cook for 3 to 5 minutes per side, until each side is evenly browned. Transfer the roast to the slow cooker.

Pour the beef broth into the pot and bring it to a boil over medium-high heat for about 1 minute, scraping the bottom of the pot with a wooden spoon to deglaze the brown bits. Momentarily remove the pot from the burner to pour in the red wine, then return the pot to the stove. Reduce the heat and stir in the Worcestershire sauce, Dijon mustard, garlic, parsley, rosemary, thyme, salt and pepper. Simmer, stirring occasionally, for 2 to 3 minutes. Allow the broth mixture to slightly cool and then pour it over the contents of the slow cooker. Cover the slow cooker and cook on low for 8 to 10 hours, or on high for 5 to 6 hours, until the roast and vegetables are tender.

Transfer the roast and the vegetables to a serving platter. Cover the platter with aluminum foil and keep it warm in an oven set to low (200°F [93°C]). Use a large spoon to skim any excess fat from the surface of the liquids in the slow cooker, and strain the pan juices through a fine-mesh sieve into a medium saucepan. Heat the saucepan over medium-high heat and bring the juices to a boil. In a small bowl, mix the cornstarch and the water until smooth. Continuously whisk the pan juices in the saucepan while slowly pouring in the cornstarch slurry. Reduce the heat to a simmer and cook for 1 to 2 minutes, stirring occasionally, until the gravy has thickened. Stir using the balsamic vinegar, if using, and season the gravy to taste with additional salt and pepper, and serve it over the roast and vegetables.

# APPLE-DIJON PORK LOIN

This tender, juicy pork loin tastes like fall. Whether you're hosting an autumn dinner party or you need an extra main course to supplement the turkey at Thanksgiving, your guests will rave over the fork-tender pork and the sweet and savory sauce, with notes of apple cider, Dijon mustard, white wine and thyme. Served with a big green salad, this easy, elegant meal shines at both special occasions and cozy family dinners!

YIELD: 6 TO 8 SERVINGS

3 lb (1.4 kg) pork loin, trimmed

1 ½ tbsp (18 g) House Seasoning (page 193)

2 tbsp (30 ml) vegetable oil

¾ cup (180 ml) low-sodium chicken broth

¾ cup (180 ml) unsweetened apple cider (or juice)

¼ cup (60 ml) dry white wine (such as Chardonnay or Pinot Grigio)

1 tbsp (15 ml) medium-dry or dry sherry, optional

1 tbsp (15 g) Dijon mustard

2 tsp (2 g) minced fresh thyme

1 tsp (2 g) minced fresh rosemary

3 tbsp (42 g) butter

3 tbsp (24 g) all-purpose flour

2 cloves garlic, minced

Salt and freshly ground black pepper, to taste

1 tsp (5 ml) honey, optional

Pat the pork loin dry with paper towels and generously season all sides with the House Seasoning, rubbing it into the meat. Heat the vegetable oil in a large pot or Dutch oven over medium-high heat. When the oil is shimmering, add the pork loin and cook for 3 to 4 minutes per side, until each side is evenly browned. Transfer the pork loin to the slow cooker, fat-side up.

In a large measuring cup, combine the chicken broth, apple cider or apple juice, white wine, sherry (if using), Dijon mustard, thyme and rosemary. Return the pot to the stove and melt the butter over medium-low heat. Once the butter is melted, add the flour and garlic and whisk continuously for 1 minute. Gradually whisk in the chicken broth mixture, increase the heat to medium-high, and bring the mixture to a simmer, whisking continuously for several minutes, until the sauce is smooth and thick. Remove the pot from the heat, adjust the seasoning to taste with salt and pepper and stir in the honey (if using) for a slightly sweeter sauce.

Allow the sauce to cool for a few minutes and then pour it over the pork loin in the slow cooker. Cover the slow cooker and cook on low for 2 to 4 hours, until the center of the pork loin reaches 145°F (63°C) on an instant-read thermometer. Transfer the pork loin to a cutting board, tent it with aluminum foil and allow it to rest for 15 minutes before slicing and serving with the sauce.

# CITRUS-GLAZED CORNISH HENS

It's hard to believe that such a gorgeous recipe can come out of the slow cooker. How special will your holiday guests (or weeknight three-year-old) feel when you present them with these exquisite, glossy Cornish hens? Four small hens should fit just perfectly in a large oval slow cooker. And just so you're prepared, the hens will release a lot of liquid as they cook and, as a result, will be practically swimming by the end of the cooking time. That's okay! Simply drain them before broiling, where the skin will crisp and they'll pick up sweet and puckery citrus flavor thanks to a simple, lovely glaze.

### YIELD: 4 SERVINGS

4 small Cornish game hens, thawed (1 ¼ to 1 ½ lb [567 to 680 g] each)

4 tbsp (56 g) butter, melted

Salt and freshly ground black pepper, to taste

¼ cup (60 ml) low-sodium chicken broth

¾ cup (177 ml) honey

⅓ cup (80 ml) low-sodium soy sauce

⅓ cup (80 ml) freshly squeezed orange juice

¼ cup (60 ml) freshly squeezed lime juice

3 tbsp (24 g) cornstarch plus 3 tbsp (45 ml) water

Pat the hens dry with paper towels, brush their skins all over with the butter and generously sprinkle them with the salt and pepper to taste. Arrange the hens upright in a large oval slow cooker, necks facing down with the breasts facing the center of the slow cooker. Pour the chicken broth into the bottom of the slow cooker. Cover the slow cooker and cook on low for 5 to 7 hours, until the juices run clear, not pink, where the leg pulls away from the body and an instant-read thermometer inserted into the thickest part of the thigh registers 165°F (74°C), without touching the bone.

Just before the hens are done, combine the honey, soy sauce, orange juice and lime juice in a small saucepan over medium heat. Bring the mixture to a boil, stirring occasionally. In a small bowl, mix the cornstarch and water until smooth. Whisk the sauce continuously while slowly pouring in the cornstarch slurry. Reduce the heat to a simmer and cook for 1 to 2 minutes, stirring occasionally, until the glaze is thick and glossy. Remove from the heat and cover the saucepan to keep the glaze warm.

Position an oven rack 6 inches (15 cm) below the heating element and preheat the broiler. Line a large, rimmed baking sheet with aluminum foil, drain the liquids out of the hens and carefully transfer them to the baking sheet, breast-side up. Generously sprinkle the hens with salt and pepper. Broil for a few minutes, until the skin begins to crisp and brown. Remove the hens from the oven, thickly coat each one with citrus glaze and return them to the broiler for a couple more minutes, until the glaze is bubbly. Allow the hens to rest for 10 minutes before serving with the remaining glaze.

# HONEY MUSTARD LEG OF LAMB

All tied up like a pretty package, boneless leg of lamb fits perfectly and cooks beautifully in the slow cooker. Coated with a glaze of honey, Dijon mustard and rosemary, this lamb turns out juicy and tender, making for a memorable celebratory meal.

### YIELD: 4 TO 6 SERVINGS

3 lb (1.4 kg) boneless leg of lamb, trimmed and tied with butcher's string or left in netting

House Seasoning (page 193), to taste

2 tbsp (30 ml) vegetable oil

½ cup (120 ml) low-sodium chicken broth

6 cloves garlic, minced

¼ cup (60 ml) honey

2 tbsp (30 g) Dijon mustard

2 tbsp (30 ml) extra-virgin olive oil

2 tbsp (10 g) minced fresh rosemary, plus more for serving

1 tbsp (15 ml) freshly squeezed lemon juice

1 tsp (6 g) salt

Freshly ground black pepper, to taste

Pat the lamb dry with paper towels and generously season both sides with the House Seasoning, rubbing it into the meat. Heat the oil in a large pot or Dutch oven over medium-high heat. Once the oil is shimmering, add the lamb and cook for 3 to 5 minutes per side, until every side is evenly browned. Transfer the lamb to a large slow cooker.

Pour the chicken broth into the pot and bring it to a boil over medium-high heat for about 1 minute, scraping the bottom of the pot with a wooden spoon to deglaze the brown bits. Allow the broth to slightly cool and then pour it over the lamb in the slow cooker.

In a medium bowl, combine the garlic, honey, Dijon, olive oil, rosemary, lemon juice, salt and pepper. Pour the mixture over the lamb and rub it into the meat, turning the lamb to evenly coat it. Cover the slow cooker and cook on low for 6 to 8 hours, until the lamb is very tender.

Transfer the lamb to a platter, tent it with aluminum foil, and allow it to rest for 15 minutes. Use a large spoon to skim any excess fat from the surface of the liquids in the slow cooker, then strain the juices through a fine-mesh sieve into a medium bowl or measuring cup. Serve the warm lamb sprinkled with rosemary and drizzled with the juices from the slow cooker.

# GARLIC "ROASTED" WHOLE CHICKEN

Classic roasted chicken is extremely underrated for being so indescribably delicious. And surprisingly, preparing it in the slow cooker makes it *so easy*! While it's not exactly possible to roast something in the slow cooker, the flavor of this garlic-seasoned bird will make you believe otherwise. The juicy meat practically falls off the bone and a quick jaunt under the broiler crisps up the skin. As for the root veggies, they soak up the savory juices pouring off the chicken as it cooks, infusing them with flavor. An impressive holiday dinner or a simple weeknight supper: the choice is yours, and it will be delightful either way!

YIELD: 4 SERVINGS

1 lb (454 g) red potatoes, cut into 1 ½-inch (4-cm) pieces

6 medium carrots, peeled and cut into 1-inch (2.5-cm) pieces

1 medium yellow onion, sliced ½-inch (13-mm) thick

8 cloves garlic, divided, minced

1 ½ tbsp (18 g) House Seasoning (page 193), plus more for seasoning vegetables

4 tbsp (56 g) butter, at room temperature

4 to 5 lb (1.8 to 2.3 kg) roasting chicken, bag of giblets removed

Freshly ground black pepper, to taste

Combine the potatoes, carrots, onions and 4 cloves minced garlic in the bottom of a large oval slow cooker. Generously sprinkle the root vegetables with the House Seasoning, to taste.

In a small bowl, combine the butter, the remaining 4 cloves minced garlic and the 1 ½ tablespoons (18 g) House Seasoning until smooth. Slip spoonfuls of the garlic butter under the chicken skin and on the breasts and thighs, and gently smooth the top of the skin to spread out the butter in a thin layer. Spread any remaining butter over the outside of the chicken. Sprinkle the chicken with freshly ground black pepper and place it on the bed of vegetables in the slow cooker.

Cover the slow cooker and cook on low for 4 to 6 hours, until the chicken breast registers 165°F (74°C) on an instant-read thermometer, the thighs register 175°F (80°C), and the juices run clear, not pink, where the chicken leg pulls away from the body. Position an oven rack 8 inches (20 cm) below the heating element and preheat the broiler. Line a large, rimmed baking sheet with heavy-duty aluminum foil and carefully transfer the chicken to it. Broil the chicken for 5 to 10 minutes, until the skin begins to crisp and brown. Remove the chicken from the oven, tent it with aluminum foil and allow it to rest for 15 minutes before carving. Serve the chicken with the vegetables on the side and the pan juices spooned over the top.

### Samantha's Tip

If your chicken is done cooking on the shorter side of the suggested cooking time, your veggies may not be totally tender yet. If this is the case, increase the temperature of the slow cooker to high as soon as the chicken comes out, and then cover the slow cooker again and cook the veggies while the chicken broils and rests.

# TURKEY AND WILD RICE SOUP

Come the end of November, I annually ask myself the same post-Thanksgiving question, as do countless others across our great country: What the heck do I do with all of this leftover turkey? The majority of the time, that answer comes in the form of soup, because, let's face it, there's nothing more comforting and filling on a chilly fall day.

If turkey is considered the lead actor in this soup, then wild rice has the most important supporting role. Over the long cooking time, it softens and breaks down, lending the soup thickness and texture. I like to stir in some half-and-half before serving to add a touch of richness to the soup, and sometimes I even garnish it with minced fresh herbs if I happen to have any leftover from Thanksgiving. And if there's nary a speck of leftover turkey to be found? Well, lucky for us all, this soup is equally dandy with chicken.

YIELD: 6 TO 8 SERVINGS

3 medium carrots, peeled and cut into ¼-inch (6-mm) thick slices

½ medium yellow onion, finely chopped

3 medium stalks celery, finely chopped

5 cloves garlic, minced

1 cup (180 g) uncooked wild rice or wild rice–brown rice mix

1 ½ tbsp (18 g) House Seasoning (page 193)

2 tsp (3 g) Poultry Seasoning (page 194)

2 dried bay leaves

10 cups (2.4 L) low-sodium chicken broth or Homemade Turkey Stock (page 195)

4 cups (560 g) chopped cooked turkey or chicken

1 cup (240 ml) half-and-half

Salt and freshly ground black pepper, to taste

Combine the carrots, onion, celery, garlic, wild rice, House Seasoning, Poultry Seasoning, bay leaves and broth in a large slow cooker. Cover the slow cooker and cook on low for 5 to 7 hours, or on high for 3 to 4 hours, until the vegetables and rice are tender. Stir in the chopped turkey or chicken and the half-and-half. Cover the slow cooker and cook on high for 30 minutes. Discard the bay leaves. Adjust the seasoning to taste with salt and pepper.

# CHEESY POTATO SOUP WITH HAM

The last thing I feel like doing the day after cooking a big, elaborate meal is spending another long day in the kitchen. That's why I'm all about a post-holiday recipe that takes just a few minutes to assemble and then requires no further thought until hours later, when it's ready to eat! Leftover Easter, Thanksgiving or Christmas ham is put to good use in this thick and creamy soup. If your ham is particularly salty, you can start with only 1 teaspoon (4 g) House Seasoning and then add more to taste once the soup is done. And *pssst* . . . if you still have ham left after whipping up a slow cooker full of this soup, consider making some Chicken Cordon Bleu Soup (page 84) tomorrow.

YIELD: 6 TO 8 SERVINGS

---

3 lb (1.4 kg) potatoes, peeled and cut into 1 ½-inch (4-cm) cubes

3 cloves garlic, minced

6 cups (1.4 L) low-sodium chicken broth

2 tsp (8 g) House Seasoning (page 193)

1 cup (240 ml) half-and-half

1 cup (4 oz [113 g]) shredded extra-sharp cheddar cheese, plus more for serving

1 ½ cups (216 g) diced ham, cut into ½-inch (13-mm) pieces

Salt and freshly ground black pepper, to taste

Combine the potatoes, garlic, chicken broth and House Seasoning in a large slow cooker. Cover the slow cooker and cook on low for 6 to 8 hours, or on high for 3 to 4 hours, until the potatoes are very tender.

Using a slotted spoon, transfer about half of the cooked potatoes to a plate and set aside. Use an immersion blender to purée the remaining potatoes until smooth. Stir in the half-and-half, cheddar, ham and reserved potatoes. If desired, thin out the soup with additional broth or half-and-half, and season to taste with salt and pepper. Cover the slow cooker and cook on low for 10 minutes, until the soup is heated through (but not too long or the soup may start to darken around the edges). Stir the soup well before serving it garnished with extra cheese.

# BLACK-EYED PEAS WITH BACON

In the South, January 1 traditionally means cooking up a big pot of black-eyed peas since, according to legend, eating black-eyed peas on New Year's Day brings luck and prosperity in the upcoming year. However, seeing as how black-eyed peas have admittedly never been my favorite, I would usually just choke down a spoonful to ring in the New Year and consider it good. But when I had a family of my own, I had to figure out a way to make this annual tradition more enjoyable. And so I did, unlocking bacon, garlic and thyme as the secret ingredients for black-eyed peas that are not only tolerable, but downright tasty!

YIELD: 4 TO 6 SERVINGS

12 slices bacon, divided (about 12 oz [340 g] total)

1 lb (454 g) dried black-eyed peas, picked over, rinsed and drained

4 cloves garlic, minced

1 cup (40 g) minced fresh parsley, divided

2 tsp (2 g) dried thyme

4 dried bay leaves

Freshly ground black pepper, to taste

8 cups (2 L) low-sodium chicken broth

Salt, to taste

To cook the bacon, position the oven rack in the center of the oven and preheat the oven to 400°F (204°C). Cover a large, rimmed baking sheet with heavy-duty aluminum foil and line it with the bacon. Cook the bacon for 15 to 20 minutes, or until it is crispy. Use a fork or tongs to remove the bacon to a paper towel–lined plate to drain. Discard the bacon grease and chop the bacon. Cover and refrigerate half of the chopped bacon, and put the rest of it in the bottom of a large slow cooker. Add the black-eyed peas, garlic, ½ cup (20 g) of the parsley, thyme, bay leaves and pepper to the slow cooker. Pour in the chicken broth and stir to combine. Cover the slow cooker and cook on low for 6 to 8 hours, until the black-eyed peas are tender. Discard the bay leaves. Season with salt and pepper to taste, and stir in the remaining ½ cup (20 g) parsley. Serve bowls of black-eyed peas topped with the reserved chopped bacon after reheating it.

# HOMEMADE SEASONINGS AND STOCKS

## Save Money and Time While Controlling the Ingredients

You've probably noticed that just about every recipe in this cookbook calls for House Seasoning, and for good reason—it enhances savory recipes with a neutral enough flavor to complement just about any cuisine, it saves time as opposed to measuring out four different common spices every time you cook, and you know exactly what's in it because—hey!—you made it yourself. As a bonus, it only takes a minute to mix up a big batch and it will last indefinitely in your spice cabinet.

But in addition to House Seasoning, the recipes in this cookbook include a few other homemade blends that can be found in this chapter, namely Italian Seasoning (page 193), Poultry Seasoning (page 194) and Taco Seasoning (page 194). I use these blends so often that I house them in reusable spice shakers. They have a front-row spot in my spice cabinet, as I reach for them frequently and refill them as soon as they run out.

If you already have a comparable store-bought seasoning blend in your kitchen—Italian seasoning, for example—you can certainly still use it when a recipe in this cookbook calls for it. But once you run out, I highly recommend mixing up your own fresh, homemade blend! If you want to start out with a smaller batch of these seasoning blends, feel free to cut any of the recipes in half.

Just two words of caution: First, be sure that you buy high-quality, all-natural base herbs and spices for mixing up your blends. And second, if your comparable store-bought herb blend looks like it's been ground into a fine powder, it's not going to be equivalent to the herb blends in this chapter, in which the dried herbs have not been ground. So if a recipe in this cookbook calls for Poultry Seasoning (page 194) and you plan on using a store-bought *ground* poultry seasoning, you will need to use *less* than the amount called for in the recipe, or the flavor will end up too strong.

Another common ingredient in many slow cooker recipes is broth or stock. So to turn leftover bones and vegetable scraps into a nourishing base for your favorite soups and stews, this chapter closes with recipes for Homemade Chicken or Turkey Stock (page 195), Homemade Beef Stock (page 196) and Homemade Vegetable Broth (page 197). Get ready to feel domestic, y'all.

# HOUSE SEASONING

You'll reach for this flavorful, all-around spice blend just about every time you cook!

YIELD: APPROXIMATELY ¾ CUP (120 G)

---

¼ cup (60 g) fine sea salt (I prefer Redmond Real Salt brand)

¼ cup (35 g) garlic powder

2 tbsp (16 g) onion powder

1 tbsp (6 g) black pepper

Combine the sea salt, garlic powder, onion powder and pepper in a small bowl and store the House Seasoning in an airtight container.

### Samantha's Tip

If you ever run out of House Seasoning and you need some for a recipe but you don't have enough individual spices left to make another batch, 1 tablespoon (12 g) House Seasoning is roughly equivalent to 1 teaspoon (6 g) salt, 1 teaspoon (3 g) garlic powder, ½ teaspoon onion powder and ¼ teaspoon pepper.

# ITALIAN SEASONING

Jazz up your favorite Italian cuisine with this versatile blend of herbs, perfect for flavoring everything from lasagna to spaghetti, marinara sauce to pizza sauce.

YIELD: APPROXIMATELY ¾ CUP (30 G)

---

¼ cup (7 g) dried parsley

¼ cup (8 g) dried basil

¼ cup (8 g) dried oregano

2 tbsp (6 g) dried thyme

1 tsp (2 g) dried rosemary

Combine the parsley, basil, oregano, thyme and rosemary in a small bowl and store the Italian Seasoning in an airtight container.

# POULTRY SEASONING

This blend of herbs and spices complements chicken or turkey entrées as well as a variety of soups and stews.

YIELD: APPROXIMATELY ½ CUP (25 G)

---

3 tbsp (5 g) dried sage

2 tbsp (6 g) dried thyme

1 tbsp (5 g) dried rosemary

1 tbsp (2 g) dried marjoram

2 tsp (5 g) ground nutmeg

1 tsp (2 g) freshly ground black pepper

Combine the sage, thyme, rosemary, marjoram, nutmeg and pepper in a small bowl and store the Poultry Seasoning in an airtight container.

# TACO SEASONING

This zesty blend of spices is not only perfect for tacos, but it's also a delicious way to flavor a multitude of Mexican and Tex-Mex recipes.

YIELD: APPROXIMATELY ½ CUP (85 G)

---

¼ cup (29 g) chili powder

2 tbsp (13 g) ground cumin

1 ½ tbsp (24 g) fine sea salt (I prefer Redmond Real Salt brand)

2 tsp (4 g) freshly ground black pepper

2 tsp (6 g) paprika

1 ½ tsp (5 g) garlic powder

1 tsp (2 g) onion powder

1 tsp (1 g) dried Mexican oregano

Combine the chili powder, cumin, sea salt, pepper, paprika, garlic powder, onion powder and Mexican oregano in a small bowl and store the Taco Seasoning in an airtight container.

# HOMEMADE CHICKEN OR TURKEY STOCK

Richly flavored Homemade Chicken or Turkey Stock makes a wonderful base for soups, stews and gravies. But the real beauty of this recipe is its flexibility! In other words, use whatever you've got. Poultry carcasses, unused gizzards, leftover vegetable scraps, aromatics—just about anything is fair game. If you're going to make turkey stock the day after Thanksgiving, for example, save all of the peels and scraps and leftover herbs as you prepare your dishes for the big meal. Don't worry about pretty veggies for your stock—a quick scrub is all they need. And don't forget the apple cider vinegar, which pulls the nutrients out of the bones. I think you'll be amazed at how throwing some ugly, otherwise useless ingredients into the slow cooker can turn into such lovely liquid gold.

YIELD: APPROXIMATELY 2 ½ QUARTS (2 L)

3 to 4 lb (1.4 to 1.8 kg) chicken or turkey bones, skin and/or carcasses, plus any unused bits such as cooked or raw necks and gizzards

2 to 3 cups (260 to 390 g) vegetable scraps (onion and garlic skins, celery tops, carrot peel, herb stems, etc.)

3 dried bay leaves

12 whole black peppercorns

1 tsp (6 g) salt, optional

2 tbsp (30 ml) apple cider vinegar

Water, as needed

IF YOU DON'T HAVE ANY (OR ENOUGH) VEGETABLE SCRAPS, YOU MAY ADD:

1 medium unpeeled onion, quartered

6 unpeeled cloves garlic, smashed

2 medium unpeeled carrots, chopped into thirds

2 medium stalks celery with tops, chopped into thirds

Fresh herb sprigs or bunches

Combine the chicken or turkey pieces, vegetables, bay leaves, peppercorns, salt (if using), apple cider vinegar and enough water to cover the other ingredients in a large oval slow cooker. Cover the slow cooker and cook on low for 8 to 10 hours. If you are home, you may skim any foam from the surface of the stock every few hours and discard it.

Turn off the slow cooker, allow the stock to cool for a bit, and pour through a strainer into a large bowl or stockpot, discarding all of the solids. Chill the stock overnight. The next day, remove the fat that has solidified on the surface. Either refrigerate the stock in an airtight container if the stock is to be used in the next 2 to 3 days, or transfer it to freezer-safe containers and freeze for 2 to 3 months.

## Samantha's Tip

When making stock or broth, fill the slow cooker with water to 1-inch (25-mm) below the top edge of the slow cooker.

# HOMEMADE BEEF STOCK

Making homemade beef stock is quite different than making homemade chicken or turkey stock. First off, a specific type of bone is required—the kind that's filled with marrow in the center—and it's likely that you'll have to ask your butcher for such bones. Just explain that you need beef shanks or a similar type of marrow bone for making beef stock, and that the bones should be cut to a length that will fit in your slow cooker. Another important step in making beef stock is that the bones should be roasted before putting them in the slow cooker in order to bring out a deep, beefy color and flavor in the stock. The beef stock will need to be skimmed as it cooks, and there will be lots of interesting blobs and globs to strain after it's done. Once it's strained and cooled, don't be surprised at its gelatin-like consistency (thanks, bone marrow!), because once reheated, it will become broth-like again and its amazing flavor and nourishing properties will more than make up for all of that work.

YIELD: APPROXIMATELY 1 ½ TO 2 QUARTS (1 ½ L TO 2 L)

---

3 lb (1.4 kg) beef marrow bones (such as beef shanks)

Water, as needed

2 medium unpeeled onions, quartered

4 unpeeled cloves garlic, smashed

3 medium unpeeled carrots, chopped into thirds

2 medium stalks celery with tops, chopped into thirds

Fresh herb sprigs or bunches

3 dried bay leaves

12 whole black peppercorns

1 tsp (6 g) salt, optional

¼ cup (60 ml) apple cider vinegar

Preheat the oven to 400°F (204°C). Place the beef marrow bones in a large, deep roasting pan lined with heavy-duty aluminum foil. Roast the bones for 45 minutes, flipping them halfway through. Transfer the bones to a large oval slow cooker. Deglaze the hot roasting pan with a ½ cup (120 ml) water, scrape up the brown bits and pour the water into the slow cooker. Add the onions, garlic, carrots, celery, herbs, bay leaves, peppercorns, salt, apple cider vinegar and enough water to cover the other ingredients in the slow cooker. Cover the slow cooker and cook on low for 12 to 24 hours. If you are home, you may skim any foam from the surface of the stock every few hours and discard it.

Turn off the slow cooker, allow the stock to cool for a bit and pour it through a strainer into a large bowl or stockpot, discarding all of the solids. Chill it overnight. The next day, remove the fat that has solidified on the surface. Either refrigerate the stock in an airtight container if the stock is to be used in the next 2 to 3 days, or transfer it to freezer-safe containers and freeze for 2 to 3 months.

### Samantha's Tip
When making stock or broth, fill the slow cooker with water to 1-inch (25-mm) below the top edge of the slow cooker.

# HOMEMADE VEGETABLE BROTH

Homemade vegetable broth is infinitely customizable. I could basically just say, "Fill your slow cooker with a bunch of vegetables and/or vegetable scraps, toss in some aromatics, fill with water, and cook all day." And then, *voilà*! Effortless vegetable broth! I'll give you some parameters below, but just know that you can use pretty much whatever floats your boat (although mild vegetables work better than something with an overpowering flavor, like broccoli). If you're feeling particularly frugal and industrious, you can even save your vegetable scraps for a while—storing them in a bag in the freezer and adding to them as you have more scraps—and then make a batch of vegetable broth once the bag is full.

YIELD: APPROXIMATELY 2 ½ QUARTS (2.5 L)

5 to 6 cups (650 to 780 g) vegetable scraps (onion and garlic skins, celery tops, carrot peel, herb stems, pepper stems, potato and sweet potato peels, asparagus ends, bottoms and tops of leeks and so on)

Fresh herb sprigs or bunches

3 dried bay leaves

12 whole black peppercorns

1 tsp (6 g) salt, optional

Water, as needed

IF YOU DON'T HAVE ANY (OR ENOUGH) VEGETABLE SCRAPS, YOU MAY ADD:

2 medium unpeeled onions, quartered

6 unpeeled cloves garlic, smashed

3 medium unpeeled carrots, chopped into thirds

2 medium stalks celery with tops, chopped into thirds

1 large tomato, quartered

8 oz (227 g) mushrooms, cleaned

Combine the vegetables, herbs, bay leaves, peppercorns, salt (if using) and enough water to cover the other ingredients in a large oval slow cooker. Cover the slow cooker and cook on low for 8 to 10 hours.

Turn off the slow cooker, allow the stock to cool for a bit and pour it through a strainer into a large bowl or stockpot, discarding all of the solids. Either refrigerate the stock in an airtight container if it is to be used in the next 2 to 3 days, or transfer it to freezer-safe containers and freeze for 2 to 3 months.

## Samantha's Tip

When making stock or broth, fill the slow cooker with water to 1-inch (25-mm) below the top edge of the slow cooker.

# ACKNOWLEDGMENTS

When I hesitantly hit "publish" on that first *Five Heart Home* blog post over three years ago, I never imagined that it would lead me here. Initially, my husband was the only one who knew about my blog. Then a few family members and friends found out about it. At some point thereafter, I was shocked and elated to discover that I had over one hundred visitors *in the same day*! And now? Well, I'm humbled and honored by the previously unfathomable number of visitors and regular followers who stop by to read, comment and make my recipes every month. As for publishing a real-life, actual cookbook, I'm still pinching myself! None of this would have been possible, however, without so many others.

To my husband, Jason—thank you for your unwavering love and support, through this cookbook project and always. You're my best friend and I can invariably count on you to be my number one fan. You encourage me when I feel discouraged, you believe in me when I don't believe in myself and you take care of me and everyone else. I love you, I appreciate you and I'm beyond blessed to be navigating this crazy life with you.

To my three beautiful, sweet, smart, precious children, Grant, Reid and Annie—thank you for filling my heart with more love and joy than I ever thought possible. I'm so proud of each one of you, and it is an honor and a privilege to be your mama. Thank you for being my willing (and blatantly honest) taste testers, and thank you for being patient with me as I do my best to juggle everything. Not to steal a line from a cheesy '90s ballad, but everything I do, I do it for you.

Thank you to my parents for being such shining examples that hard work and determination (with a touch of sheer stubbornness) pay off. Thank you to my brother for always making me laugh with your dry and witty sense of humor. Thank you to my in-laws for loving me as one of your own from the very beginning. Thank you to the rest of my family and friends for your love, support and encouragement throughout my life. I'm so lucky to call you "my people." And to those who acted as my special slow cooker recipe testers? Y'all played an integral role in the creation of this cookbook, and to say that I appreciate you would be a huge understatement.

Thank you to my amazing, faithful blog readers and followers. This cookbook is because of you and for you. I'm so grateful that you not only make my recipes, but that you let me know when you enjoy them . . . and then you come back for more! Thank you to Page Street Publishing for reaching out to me and collaborating together on a cookbook with such a solid, useful concept. It has been a pleasure working with your team, and I'm very thankful for and humbled by this opportunity.

Last but certainly not least, I am ever thankful to God for each and every one of the wonderful people and amazing blessings in my life.

# ABOUT THE AUTHOR

**SAMANTHA SKAGGS** is the founder, recipe developer, photographer, writer, inept tech support and slightly sarcastic voice behind *Five Heart Home*, a food blog that focuses on quick and easy, family-friendly, real-food recipes. Since *Five Heart Home* was first launched in June 2013, Samantha has enjoyed an ever-growing following of loyal readers. Her work has been featured in print publications such as *Cooking Light* magazine and the *Austin American Statesman* and on online sites such as Country Living, People, All You, Delish, MSN, BuzzFeed, Huffington Post, TODAY, PBS, The Kitchn, Walmart, TipHero, PopSugar and many more.

Samantha's former occupations include seven years as a first-grade teacher and a brief stint as a textbook editor. But her favorite job ever is the one in which her subordinates fondly (and repeatedly) refer to her as Mama, a role that she currently juggles with that of food blogger. Samantha lives in the beautiful Texas Hill Country with her handsome hubby, two energetic boys and sweet baby girl. When she's not wrangling children or busying herself in the kitchen, you will likely find her watching college football (*whoop!*), using obsessive amounts of hand sanitizer or enjoying the occasional frosty margarita and large bowl of queso.

# INDEX